OUT OF THE BLUE

HELEN DUNMORE

OUT OF THE BLUE

POEMS 1975-2001

BLOODAXE BOOKS

ISBN: 1 85224 576 X

First published 2001 by
Bloodaxe Books Ltd,
Highgreen,
Tarset,
Northumberland NE48 1RP.

Bloodaxe Books Ltd acknowledges
the financial assistance of Northern Arts.

Cover printing by J. Thomson Colour Printers Ltd, Glasgow.

Printed in Great Britain by
Cromwell Press Ltd, Trowbridge, Wiltshire.

CONTENTS

FROM *Recovering a Body* (1994)

ACKNOWLEDGEMENTS

This book includes all the poems which Helen Dunmore wishes to keep in print from her previous Bloodaxe collections *The Apple Fall* (1983), *The Sea Skater* (1986), *The Raw Garden* (1988), *Short Days, Long Nights: New & Selected Poems* (1991), *Recovering a Body* (1994) and *Bestiary* (1997), together with a new collection, *Out of the Blue* (2001), and a selection of poems for children previously published in *Secrets* (Bodley Head, 1994).

Acknowledgements are due to the editors of the following publications in which some of the previously uncollected poems in the *Out of the Blue* section first appeared: *The Guardian, The Independent, Poetry Review, The Printer's Devil, Proof, Wading through the Deep Water* (Coychurch Press, 2000). 'Jacob's Drum' and 'Mr Lear's Ring' were first broadcast on *Poetry Proms* on BBC Radio 3. 'Ice Coming' was commissioned for the Salisbury Festival. 'Piers Plowman: The Crucifixion and Harrowing of Hell' was commissioned and broadcast by BBC Radio 3.

OUT OF THE BLUE

(2001)

Out of the Blue

Speak to me in the only language
I understand, help me to see
as you saw the enemy plane
pounce on you out of the sun:
one flash, cockling metal. Done.

Done for, they said, as he spun earthward
to the broad chalk bosom of England.
Done for and done.

You are the pilot of this poem,
you speaks its language, thumbs-up
to the tall dome of June.
Even when you long to bail out
you'll stay with the crate.

Done for, they said, as his leather jacket
whipped through the branches.
Done for and done.

Where are we going and why so happy?
We ride the sky and the blue,
we are thumbs up, both of us
even though you are the owner
of that long-gone morning,
and I only write the poem.

You own that long-gone morning.
Solo, the machine-gun stitched you.
One flash did for you.
Your boots hit the ground
ploughing a fresh white scar in the downland.

They knew before they got to him,
from the way he was lying
done for, undone.

But where are we going?
You come to me out of the blue
strolling the springy downland
done for, thumbs up, oil on your hands.

The man on the roof

When my grandmother died my father eulogised her.
There she was, coming home with the pram
and her crowd of children
when something strange in the light
or its impediment getting at her from heaven
made her look up to see one of her children –
her eldest child, her son, him –

up on the roof, riding the horse of the homestead
with wild heels, daring her to defy him
and get him down. She got him down
with a word, as he remembers it,
her lovely penny-pale face looking up at his
from the path where her children swarmed and shouted
and it was this

he remembered when her coffin lay under his hands:
the roof, and his coming down.

When our priest died I remembered him
up on the roof, mending a tile
– a little job on hand, and a hammer
and air of busyness to keep him busy
while he pretended not to be pretending
to ride the roof in its wild beauty
over the unfamilied air of Liscannor

and half-way to America. Maybe.
Or maybe merely tapping the tile in
like a good workman.
'How beautiful it was up on the roof,'
he said to the people at Mass.

My father touched his mother's coffin
and did not say how golden her hair was.
Even I remember how golden it was
when the grey knot was undone.

Now they are gone into the ground,
both of them. They are riding on the roof,
their wild heels daring us to defy them,
and we are here on the ground
penny-pale and gaping.
They will not tell
how beautiful it is. I will not ask them.

Giraffes in Hull

Walking at all angles
to where the sky ends,
wantons with crane-yellow necks
and scarlet legs
stepping eastward, big eyes
supping the horizon.

Watch them as they go, the giraffes
breast-high to heaven,
herding the clouds.
Only Hull has enough sky for them.

Jacob's drum

This is Jacob's drum
how he beats on it   how he fights on it
how he splits every crack of the house
how he booms
how he slams
hair wet-feathered   sweat gathering
red-face Jacob throwing his money down
all on the drum   his one number
beating   repeating

O Jacob
don't let go of it
don't let anyone take your drum
don't let anyone of all of them
who want you to be drumless
beating your song on nothing
Jacob   they'd do it
believe them

it's time   they say
to put your drum away

do you remember the glow-worm Jacob?
how we looked and nearly touched it
but you didn't want to hurt it?
I thought it was electric

some trash a child dropped
some flake of neon
stuck to a rock

don't put your finger on the light
you said   and I stood still then
glow-worm   Jacob   remember it
I had the word but it was you
who told me it was living

and now I say to anyone
don't touch Jacob's drum

That old cinema of memory

O that old cinema of memory
with the same films always showing.
The censor has been at work again.
Is he protecting me, or am I protecting him?
This trailer's a horror, I won't watch it,
this one makes my heart burn with longing,
this is a mist of interrupted shapes
urgently speaking, just out of earshot –
experimental, I call it.

The projectionist should be on double time.
He's got a kid in with him, they're so bored
they play Brag rather than watch the screen.
The ice-cream girl's tired of pacing the aisles.
She rests her thumbs in the tray-straps, and dreams.

It's a rainy afternoon in Goole
and this cinema's the last refuge
for men in macs and kids bunking off school.
They yawn, pick their nails and dream
by text-message. Look at the screen,
it says CU, CU, CU.

Depot

The panting of buses through caves of memory:
school bus with boys tossing off
in the back seat when I was eight,
knowing the words, not knowing
what it was those big boys were murkily doing,
and the conductor with fierce face
yelling down farm lanes at kids as they ran
Can you not get yourselves up in the morning?

The sway of buses into town
the way the unlopped branches of lime
knocked like sticks against railings,
the way women settled laps and bags,
shut their eyes, breathed out on a cigarette,
gave themselves to nothing for ten minutes
as someone else drove the cargo of life,
until the conductor broke their drowse
in a flurry of one-liners,
and they found coin in their fat purses.

A lorry-load of stuff

It was the green lorry with its greasy curtain
like a leather apron,
backing into the lane behind the terrace
for a lorry-load of stuff.

Cardboard boxes of books from the last move,
not opened since. That's thirteen years
where *A Beginner's Guide to Birdsong*
and *Marxism Matters* have not been wanted.

Two plastic caterpillars, clattering
like tongues. They were new once,
expensive enough to keep for no purpose.
The boxes exist, though they don't fit.

A turquoise baby-bath, impregnated
with the white-knuckle grip of one baby
and the fat relaxed fist of the other.
One afternoon it served as a sledge

before the proper sledge, this one
(which we also don't want). Remember those woods,
and our stopped breath that headlong
downhill with both boys crammed in front.

A proper lorry-load of stuff
needs bits of wood, likely shapes
that finally won't hold shelves up.
It needs a toddler's bike

hand-painted silver by a nine-year-old
then torn apart to make a go-kart.
If there is old food (lentils,
tins with rust-spots, onion sets

that never got planted, or could be gladioli)
so much the better. In a climate too cold
for cockroaches, you can afford to be careless
of larder shelves. And your lorry-load

is incomplete without the photographs
you kept taking, badly, from duty,
interrupting the happiest moments
as you saw them. The booty

of time, it was going to be. Lose them
to the panting of the lorry's engine
impatient now, throbbing, and to the man
parting the curtain, chucking stuff in.

Virgin with Two Cardigans

There's a stone set in the car-park wall
down at knee-level
which commends her.

There are these relics: a scrap of wool,
a lost button, an unfollowed pattern.

There is her stone, set in the car-park wall
its flinty lettering so bright cut
it would blind her.

Here, on this path, slowly, leaning
on two sticks, she still comes.
Trying to know all the new faces
she looks about her, tortoise-sweet.

How patiently she wants God to unbutton
her two cardigans,
but he is slow.

Here, buttoning her cardigans
with lumpy fingers she bungles
in the lee of a breeze-block wall.

Virgin with Pineapple
Virgin with the Globe as a Golden Ball

Virgin with Two Cardigans
pushing a pearl button
into the gnarl of its hole.

Ice coming
(after Doris Lessing)

First, the retreat of bees
lifting, heavy with the final
pollen of gorse and garden,
lugging the weight of it, like coal sacks
heaped on lorry-backs
in the ice-cream clamour of August.

The retreat of bees, lifting
all at once from city gardens –
suddenly the roses are scentless
as cold probes like a tongue,
crawling through the warm crevices
of Kew and Stepney. The ice comes
slowly, slowly, not to frighten anyone.

Not to frighten anyone. But the Snowdon
valleys are muffled with avalanche,
the Thames freezes, the Promenade des Anglais
clinks with a thousand icicles, where palms
died in a night, and the sea
of Greece stares back like stone
at the ice-Gorgon, white as a sheet.

Ice squeaks and whines. Snow slams
like a door miles off, exploding a forest
to shards and matchsticks. The glacier
is strangest, grey as an elephant,
too big to be heard. Big-foot, Gorgon –
a little mythology
rustles before it is stilled.

So it goes. Ivy, mahonia, viburnum
lift their fossilised flowers
under six feet of ice, for the bees
that are gone. As for being human
it worked once, but for now
and the foreseeable future
the conditions are wrong.

Cyclamen, blood-red

Cyclamen, blood-red, fly into winter
against the grey grain of concrete
eight floors up.
Winged, poised, intricate,

tough as old boots
flying the kite
of pure colour

season to season
under a laurel leaf
they make rebellion.

Piers Plowman
The Crucifixion & Harrowing of Hell
(from the C text)

'It is finished,' said Christ. Blood ebbed from his face.
He was wan and pitiful as a dying prisoner.
The lord of light closed his eyes to the light,
day shrank back, the sun darkened in terror;
The temple walls collapsed into rubble
solid rock split, and it seemed black night.
Earth shivered like living flesh,
the dead heard, and emerged
rising up from their deep-dug graves
to tell the world why this storm was wrenching it.
'For a bitter battle,' said one dead man walking,
'Life and Death are wrestling in the darkness
and no one knows who shall be the winner
until Sunday, when the sun rises,'
that said, he sank down
a dead man, into deep earth again.

Some said it was God's own son who died so well.
Truly this was the son of God,
Some said he was a sorcerer, and practised witchcraft,
'Let's try him, find out if he's really dead
or still alive, before they take down the body.'

There were two thieves that suffered death
on the cross beside Christ. An officer came
and broke their bones, the arms and legs on each man.
But all shrank from laying hands on Christ.
He was King and knight himself, his nature God-given,
and none had the boldness to touch him in his dying.
Only a blind knight stepped out, holding his spear
that was ground keen and sharp as a razor.
He was named Longinus, and had been blind for long years.

Despite his protests, they pushed him forward
to joust with Jesus, this blind Jew Longinus.
No one else dared, of all those standing there,
to touch Jesus or take him down for burial,
only the blind man, who struck his lance through Christ's heart.
Blood leaped down the shaft and melted the darkness
that sealed the knight's eyes. As the light shone
he knelt and cried to Christ to forgive him

'It was against my will that I wounded you,
I bleed to think of what I have done to you.
I yield to your mercy. Do what you like with me.
Take my land and my life, they belong to you.'

For a while in my dream I withdrew into the shadows
as if I would sink down into hell's darkness.
There my sight cleared, there this was revealed:
out of the west a young woman came hurrying
gentle, benign, sweet-spoken,
compassion itself shining. Mercy was her name
and as she came she stared into hell's mouth.
From the east, as it seemed in my vision,
her sister appeared, lightly stepping westward:
she was virgin, pristine, inviolable Truth,
wrapped in such virtue that she feared nothing.

When they met, Mercy and Truth together,
they asked each other about these signs and wonders
the din and darkness, and how the day dawned
and how a glow and glory lay at hell's mouth.

'I am dumbfounded, dazzled,' said Truth,
'I must go and make sense out of these mysteries.'
'No mystery,' said Mercy, 'but signs of bliss.
A virgin named Mary became a mother
though no man touched her. She conceived by the word
and touch of the holy spirit, grew great, gave birth.
Without labour or loss she brought her child into the world.
God is my witness that my tale is true
and thirty winters have passed since that child was born
who suffered and died today, about mid-day;
it is his death which has darkened the sun
and made the bright world lightless, but this eclipse has meaning:
like the sun, man shall be released from shadow
when the light of life blinds the eyes of Lucifer.
The prophets and patriarchs have preached to us
that what was lost by a tree should be won back through a tree,
and what death felled, shall be death's downfall.'

'What friend of a friend told you that?' asked Truth.
'Listen to me. This is Truth speaking.
Adam and Eve, Abraham,
all their companions, all that are human,
all those prophets and patriarchs that suffer hell's pains –
that light will never be allowed to lift them up

and have them out of hell – Mercy, stop mouthing
and hold your tongue, for I am Truth
and I tell this truth, that hell holds them.
Read Job, and let him put you right by his ruling
that hell *allows no redemption.*'

Mercy, unruffled, answered her sister.
'I have grounds for hope, hope for salvation.
Poison drives out poison, the cycle is broken
Adam and Even shall find their redemption.
Of all venoms the worst is the scorpion's.
No doctor's skill can heal the site of his sting,
until the scorpion dies, and, held to the wound
drives out its own poison, turns sting to balm.
I would lay a bet with my life as stake
that this death will undo the deathly devilment
done to Eve in the earliest days.
And as the serpent seduced and beguiled,
so grace, which made all things, will mend all things,
and trick the tricksters by holy sleight of hand.'

'Let's stop all this,' said Truth, 'I see, not far off,
Righteousness running out of the north
from the cut of the cold. Let's argue no more
for she's the eldest of us, and knows most.'
'True,' said Mercy, 'and look, from the south
Peace dressed in Patience, dancing towards us.
Love has longed for her so long, I think it must be that Love
himself has written to her. His love-letter
will enlighten us all. We'll soon know the meaning
of this light that hangs over hell.'

When Peace, clothed in Patience, came up to them,
Righteousness curtsied to Peace in her rich clothing
and begged her to say which way she was going,
and whose hearts she would lift by the loveliness of her dress.

'I am filled with longing to welcome them all,'
said Peace, 'all those who have been hidden from me
by the pollution of sin and hell's darkness,
Adam and Eve and a crowd of others,
Moses and more than I can name. Mercy shall sing
while I dance to her music: do so, dear sister!
For Jesus fought well for them, and this is joy's dawning.
Love, who is my lover, has sent me a warrant
which declares that Mercy and Peace bring freedom

to release the human race from its prison,
for Christ has changed the nature of justice
into peace and forgiveness, through his grace.
Here's the warrant,' said Peace, '*in peace I will both lay me down* –
and to prove it is binding – *and rest secure.*'

'Are you out of your mind,' asked Righteousness,
or have you been drinking?
Do you really think that light there
has power to unlock hell?
Do you really believe it can save human souls?
When the world began, God gave his judgement
that Adam and Eve and their descendants
should die, and go down to everlasting darkness
for touching the tree and its sweet fruit.
Adam broke the law of our lord and denied his love,
by eating the fruit he gave up both love and law,
followed evil and fought against reason.
– by the letter of the law it is all over,
they must suffer for ever, no prayer,
no intercession can come near them.
They chose the fruit, let them chew on it.
And as for us, sisters, let's not complain of it.
That apple bite was a landslip
which changed their landscape for ever.'

'But I shall pray for them,' Peace said, 'for the end of their pain.
Joy and suffering are twined together so tightly
that one cannot be known without the other.
Hunger means nothing to full stomachs.
If all the world were like a swan's breast,
who would know what white was?
If night never came, what would day mean,
and if God's own tongue had not tasted death
how would he tell if was sweet or sour?
A rich man, living in health and ease
would never suffer, but for the death
that comes to all, equally, inescapably.

So God, who struck the light that began life
chose to be born human, to save mankind,
and be sold into death to feel the pain of dying,
which unknits all cares and ends suffering.

*

God placed Adam in peace and plenty,
God gave him freedom to sin and to suffer
to learn through this what his happiness was.
and God challenged himself to take on Adam's nature
and know human fate in his own flesh.
He came from heaven, lived on earth, and now
will go down to hell, and discover
the depth of suffering. The dark world
opens to Christ, who lived in heaven's light.
Christ will take the human race with him
on the same journey. Their descent into evil
will lead them to know where love is.'

'Listen,' said Truth, 'I see and hear it happening.
A spirit speaks to hell and bids it unbar the gates.
Lift up your heads, O ye gates...'

A voice blazed from the light at Lucifer,
'Prince of this place, tear these gates open
for the crowned King of Glory to enter them.'
Then Satan shuddered and said to hell
'A light like this took Lazarus from us.
This is the moment of our undoing.
If this king enters, he will take mankind from us
and lead it where Lazarus has gone, and seize me.
Patriarchs and prophets warned of this
that such a lord and such a light would lead them.
Get up, Ragamoffyn, reach me those bars
from your Grandad Belial's wife-battering
and I'll stop this lord and his light.
Before this brightness blinds us, let's bar the gates,
check his course, chain our doors, stop up the chinks
so no light leaps in at the loop holes or louvers.

Ashtaroth, get the lads moving, the whole gang of them,
to defend mankind. They're ours, we'll keep them.
Hurl down the brimstone, blazing and boiling
to flay the flesh of those who come near our kingdom.
Set the crossbows and the brass cannon
and blind his troops with our ammunition.'

'Listen,' said Lucifer, 'I know this lord,
this lord and this light. From long ago I knew him.
No death can snuff out this lord, hell cannot cheat him.
Where he wishes, there he goes. But let him look out.
If he tears them away from me, he does it by force, not right.

For by right and reason, they belong to me
body and soul, the good and the evil.
For the lord of heaven himself promised it:
Adam and Eve and all their descendants
should suffer death and come to me for ever
if they touched the tree or picked the apple.
It was this same lord of light who gave the judgement,
and since he is truth itself, he must keep to it,
not tear from us what is ours, damned by justice.
We have had them with us for seven thousand winters,
legally ours, with no one arguing it.
Will he be untrue, who is truth itself?'

'True,' said Satan, 'but all the same…
You trapped them and tricked them, trampled down his Eden.
Against his law and desire you slunk onto his land
and caught Eve alone.
Woe to those who are alone!
And when you had separated her, you seduced her,
then promised them both they should become
as Gods with God, judging and knowing.
With treason and treachery you deceived them both
and brought them to break obedience through false promises.
So you got them out of Eden, and brought them here at last.
It was deception, not fair getting.

God will not be mocked,' said the Evil One.
'Watch out if you try to make a fool of him.
Our title deeds to their souls are false.
My terror is that truth will come for them.
As you mocked God's image in becoming snake
so God has deceived us in becoming man.
For God has gone about for thirty winters
in human flesh, travelling, preaching.
I sent sin to court him, and I asked him
if he were God, or God's son. He gave me a short answer.
So he's been out and about these thirty-two years.
When I saw what was happening, I plotted and planned
to stop those who hated him from martyring him.
I would have lengthened his life, for I believed
if he died, if his soul penetrated Hell
it would make an end of us all.

While his bones lived, he never rested
from his love lessons. 'Love one another' –
but the end of that love, and the aim of that law
is the end of us devils, and our downfall.

And now I see his soul come sailing towards us
in light and glory – I know this is God.
We must retreat, throw down our arms.
It would be better for us never to have been,
better to vanish from existence
than to endure the sight of this Christ.
Through your lies, Lucifer, we first lost heaven
and plunged to hell. You dragged us down.
We swallowed your lies and lost all happiness,
and now, because you had to lie again
and betray Eve, we have lost hell and earth
where we were lords and ruled everything.
Now shall the prince of this world be cast out.'

Again, that light bid the gates open. Lucifer answered
'What Lord are you?' A voice said aloud
'The lord of power and might, that made all things.
Duke of this damned place, now undo these gates
that Christ may come in, heaven's son.'
As he breathed these words, hell broke, and all Belial's bars.
No guard could keep those gates. They opened wide.
Patriarchs and prophets, the people that dwelled in darkness
sung with Saint John, 'Behold the Lamb of God'.
Lucifer blazed into blindness, and saw nothing
while those that our Lord loved flowed forth with that light.
'Here I am,' said our Lord, 'body and soul,
to claim for all the rights of body and soul.
They were made by me, they were always mine.
My law and my justice promised them
that if they ate the apple they should die,
but I never condemned them to hell for ever.
Their deadly sin came by your deception,
you got them with trickery, trickery took them.
You crept into my Eden in the shape of an adder
to steal away what I loved and looked after,
you teased and tricked them and destroyed my Eden.
The Old Law teaches that tricks will catch tricksters,
and truss them up in a web of deception.

Those that take life must lose their own lives,
the Old Law teaches. A murderer's life is exacted.
One soul must pay for another, the sin of my Crucifixion
wipes out Original Sin. For I am human,
and capable of making amends for human sin.
Through my own death, I undo death,
and I ransom all those crushed through sin,
and I trick the tricksters of hell through my grace.
So do not fool yourself, Lucifer, that I come against the law
to fetch any sinful soul by force,
but by justice and truth I ransom what is mine.

What was got with guile, is regained by grace.
As the human race died through a tree
so by a tree they shall come to life,
And your deception begins to turn
inwards, and stab your own flesh,
while my grace flourishes.
You have brewed bitterness, now swallow it.
Doctor of death, drink your own medicine.

I that am lord of life, love is my drink,
and for that drink I died today, as it seemed.
I do not drink from gold cups, or refined teaching,
only the common cup of all Christian souls.
But your drink shall be death, and deep hell your bowl.

After the great fight thirst grips me still,
my thirst for every human soul.
My thirst is so great that nothing can touch it –
all your spirits and rare vintages
will never slake it, till the grapes are ripe
and the dead wake. Ripe, and purple, and heavy-hanging
in the valley of the resurrection,
and then I shall come into my kingdom
and bring out of hell all human souls.

By right I will lead them out of this place,
all those I loved, all who believed in my coming,
but because you lied to Eve, Lucifer, you shall pay for it.'
And the lord bound Lucifer in chains.
Ashtaroth and the others hid in hell's crannies:
They did not dare even look on the lord
but let him lead forth whomever he chose
and leave behind him in hell whomever he chose.

The angels sang and swept their harps,
hundreds of angels poured out their music:
The flesh sins, the flesh atones for sin,
the flesh of God reigns as God.

Then Peace played these verses on her pipes:
'Glittering sun after rain,' sang Peace
The warmth of sun after rain-loaded clouds,
no love is sweeter, no friends dearer
than when peace comes after war.
Peace, armed with patience, puts an end to danger,
stills violence, destroys terror.'
'Truly,' said Truth, 'Here is the heart of truth.
Let us offer one another the kiss of peace.'
'And let no one say that we argue among ourselves,
for nothing is impossible to God,' said Peace.
'You speak the truth,' said Righteousness,
and she took Peace in her arms tenderly.
Mercy and Truth have met together
Justice and Peace have kissed one another.

They sang together in my dream until the day dawned
when the church-bells rang for the Resurrection,
and with that sound I awoke
and called Kit my wife and Colette my daughter,
'Get up, and honour God's resurrection,
creep to the cross, venerate it, kiss it
like the most precious jewel there is,
most worthy relic, richest on earth.
It bore our Lord's body to do us good,
and in the shadow of the cross
no ghosts can gather, no evil can live.'

Smoke

Old warriors and women
cough their glots of winter-thick phlegm
while a dog hackles for the bone
that the boy on the floor has stolen.

Whining, mithering children
in swaddles of urine-damp wool, prickling
with lice, impetigo and scabies, again
the toothache, the earache, the scabies, the glands
battling. Hush by the fire again
sing him a song, rock him again,
again, till he sleeps, still whining and wizening.

On the earth floor rocks his squat cradle
on the squat earth he has come to,
while one of the obsolete warriors
wheezes away at an instrument
made of sheep's innards.

He is a man of skills
learned painfully, not much of a singer
wheezing for the second time that evening
of the boar he killed with a dagger
of the bear with razor claws
that scooped out the face of his brother
then fell to his spear.

In song he remakes his brother
and their small play on the earth floor.
The baby cries. Smoke fills the hall,
the eyes of warriors and old women,
and nobody listens.

There's the skin of the bear on the floor
and a hearth gaping with flame
red-mouthed, then smoke hides it again.
By thirty everyone's teeth are broken –
look at that kid worrying his bone.

Bristol Docks

Ships on brown water
wings unruffling
masts steep and clean,

There goes the dredger,
there the steam crane
downcast, never used.

Tide goes wherever
tide goes,
forty foot rise
forty foot fall,
ship waiting
to clear Hotwells.

Time rises
time falls.
Two hundred years
shrink to nothing,

huge tides
shrunk to a drop
caught in a cup
where the men sip

tea, coffee
laced with rum,
talk venturing
westward, moneyward.

This is the slaver
money funded,
good money
from tradesmen's pockets,
guinea by guinea
fed into it.
Double it, treble it,
build on it.

Don't stare –
you'll cross them:
William Miller,
Isaac Elton,

Merchant Trader,
Merchant Venturer,
powerful men.

Edward Colston's
almshouses
(slaver panelled)
still standing.
Sugar houses
(easy burning)
all gone,
brown water
brown rum.

Custom House
African House
bonded warehouse
almshouse
sugar house.
Mud slack
licking its chops,
bright water
fighting to rise.

Look in their eyes.
They'll stare you down
for it takes guts
to get returns.
Investor,
speculator,
accumulator,
benefactor.

See their white wings
fledge on the Avon.
They speak of cargo,
profit-margins,
schools they've founded,
almshouses.

If you stare
at the brown water
you will see nothing,
every reflection
sucked and gone.

Slaver's gone
on savage wings,
beak preying.
Tradesmen's guineas
got their return:

coffee, cotton,
cocoa, indigo,
sugar, rum,
church windows,
fine houses,
fine tombstone
for Edward Colston,

the cry of gulls
goes after them
always lamenting,
always fresh
beaks stabbing
at their soul-flesh.

The spill

Those words like oil, loose in the world,
spilling from fingertip to fingertip
besmirching lip after lip,

the burn; the spillage of harm.
Those words like ash, mouth-warm.

Without remission

Because she told a lie, he says,
because she lied
about the hands not washed before shopping,
she had to learn,

because he wanted her to learn
the law that what he said, went,
and that was the end,
and because she was slow
she had to learn
over and over.

He was an old-fashioned teacher,
he taught her hair to lie straight,
he taught her back to bend,
he taught silence
but for the chink of coathangers
stirring in the wardrobe.

He kicked the voice out of her.
There were no words left to go
with the seven-year-old girl
soiled and bleeding,
marched along the corridor

by this man, rampant
with all he had learned.
Later, locked up once more
she called through the door to her mother
'It's all right, Mum, I'm fine.'
But she was lying.

The rain's coming in

Say we're in a compartment at night
with a yellow label on the window
and a wine bottle between your knees,

jolting as fast as the sparks
torn from night by the wheels.
Inside, the sleeping-berth is a hammock

and there I swing like a gymnast
in a cradle of jute diamonds.
Outside, the malicious hills,

where to stop is to be borne away
in the arms of a different destiny,
unprotesting. Too sleepy to do anything

but let it be. So, that oak, lightning-cracked,
shakes where the flame slashes
and kills its heart. Swooshing up air

in armfuls its branches unload
toppling beyond the rails'
hard-working parallels. Say you join me,

say your eyes are drowsy,
say you murmur, *The rain's coming in,*
pull up the strap on the window,
the rain's coming in.

As good as it gets

She comes close to perfection,
taking the man on her thigh,
sweeping him home
in a caress of glitter, that way and this,

that, this, each muscle stripped
to bulge and give. See how her hair
streams in the firmament,
see how the tent

jutting with spotlights
puts one over her, then another,
another, a spurt of white
that slicks to her thighs

while the crowd claps time,
faster and faster, wishing she'll fall
wishing she'll plunge for ever
licked all over with glitter

love-juices, spittle.
Back she comes on herself,
her bird costume flaring.
As she lets him down

you see the detail: the rosin,
the sweat that follows her spine,
the sly, deliberate spin
with which he steps onto land.

But the crowd won't stop clapping.
They want her again,
they've been translated, they're Greek,
shouting *Die now! This is as good as it gets!*

If only

If only I'd stayed up till four in the morning
and run through the dawn to watch the balloons
at the Festival ground,
and seen you as your balloon rose high
on a huff of flame, and you'd waved,
and a paper aeroplane had swooped to the ground
with your mobile number scrawled on the wings.

If only I'd known that you were crying
when you stood with your back to me
saying that it didn't matter
you'd be fine on your own.
If only I'd trusted your voice
instead of believing your words.

If only I hadn't been too late, too early,
too quick, too slow, too jealous and angry,
too eager to win
when it wasn't a game.
If only we could go back to then
and I could pick up your paper aeroplane
and call you for the very first time.

Mr Lear's Ring

Mr Lear has left a ring in his room.
Is it of value, is it an heirloom?
Should we pack it with brown paper and string
And post it after him?

He hasn't the air of a marrying man
He hasn't a husbandly air.
No, his gait is startled and sudden,
And is he quite all there?

Poor Mr Lear has left a ring in his room
And it's not of value, it's never an heirloom,
But we'll pack it with brown paper and string
And we'll send it wherever he's gone.

Fortune-teller on Church Road

Two of us on the tired pavement
with the present pushing past
into the pungent smoke of the coffee-shop,

carrier bags stuffed with cargo
from Wal-mart and Tesco.
A tree of heaven, bright yellow

spreads its leaves above the peardrop
solvent scent of ASNU VALETING SERVICES.
She looks where I'm looking

this woman who asks questions
and tells me everything I've ever done.
For twenty pounds she'll give me a golden future

for ten pounds she'll give me a silver future
for a fiver a slam of bronze.
I believe in the glow of the leaves

in the shine of car-wax, in Wal-mart
and in the whiteness of her false teeth.
She would like to lie, but whatever possesses her

won't let her. Here it comes again
clearing the coffee-smoke, thinning the cargo
of carrier bags pushing past us,

until the Saturday men and women
lose their foothold in time.
Now they are the dead walking
at the pace of long-ago film.

Sleeveless

There he stands, blind on slivovitz,
eyes closed, face beatific,
propped against the side of the coach
while two girls rub him with snow.

He goes sleeveless in the snow
as if he belongs elsewhere
in a land where blood alone
is enough to warm him.

But this isn't spring. A hyacinth's
white whip of root in a jar in November
won't stop winter. The sun will go down,
the wolves will sample the woods

and snuff his footprints. But the engine's running.
Its vibration scrubs him awake
and those girls are laughing.
In ten long easy minutes
he will have left the summit.

The point of not returning

is to go back, but never quite back.
Through all those trees I am unable
to glimpse the house. Where the new road swings,
the dark lane made for footsteps remains hidden.
Where lilac-striped convolvulus
wound its scent in the dust, new road signs
describe the route in numeral and symbol.

There is the hill, but not the right hill.
There is a blood-red rhododendron
by a breeze-block wall – but not the right wall,
and those children in a sunburned straggle
who face the oncoming traffic (thicker now),
have bought the wrong sweets at the wrong prices.
They have too much cash: they are not the right children.

The form

Clearing the mirror to see your face
I'm sure you are there.
You came into the room behind me
but when I looked you disappeared.

Look. I am breathing out mist
like a horse in winter.
The glass I almost kissed
has gone cold. Now, is it you here

sitting in your usual chair
under the light, with your Guinness poured
and the best bit of the newspaper?
Let's have a tenner on Papillon, I'm sure

he'll do it this time. You show me the form.
I put out my hand for the winnings
and take the notes which are warm
from your touch. But the mirror is cold, sparkling.

The sentence

How hushed the sentence is this morning
like snowfall: words change the landscape
by hiding what they touch.
'How is he –? Has he –?'

Bridget takes off her glasses
and rubs the red pulp of her eyelids.
The world is a treasure-house of frost
and sparkling roof-tops. A few doors down
the sentence works itself out.

A roller-blader slashes the street like an angel
with heaven-red cheeks. A fag-end smokes
in the gutter where a dog noses. Such elation!
The labour of goodbyes
goes on quietly behind windows.

With short, harsh breaths

With short, harsh breaths
and lips hitched to each syllable
you read, but not aloud.

You rise and go to the stairwell
as if to call someone. Look up
at the whitish skylight, the peace

of another rain-pocked eleven o'clock.
You are here and you want her
but she'll come no more.

You keep her letters in a box
and deal them out like patience
to lie on your breakfast table

stamps obsolete, envelope eagerly torn
by the man who once lived in your skin.
You read the postmark again.

It's September, four years after the war.
Listen. She's speaking.

The footfall

It was you I heard, your tiger pad on the stairs,
your animal eyes blazing. Now you have my face
between your paws, tiger. It's time
for the first breath. Your playful embrace.

Suddenly you take away my texture,
the sheen I've had since I was born.
My hair. You comb it out with your claws
until the gloss and colour are gone.

My skin puckers slowly. Your whiskers quiver
as I keep still between your fore-feet
while you drink my juices, and for the first time
rake the lightest glissade down my cheeks.

Time for you, tiger, to do as you want.
I heard your footfall and waited in the dark,
expecting you. When will you come?

The coffin-makers

I can't say why so many coffin-makers
have come together here. Company, maybe.
More likely jealousy bites their lips
when they see another's golden coffin
where the corpse will fit like a nut.

No doubt they swap the lids about
at dead of night, scratch the silken cheeks of the wood
so when the mourners come to watch the hammer
bounce off the nails, they'll say it's no good
and in their white clothes they'll swarm
all over the coffin-maker like angry ghosts.

There's no need for it to be like this.
They could lend their tools to one another.
They could watch each other's little shrines
in case the candle goes out. Instead they blow it out
and sourly scour the insides of another cheap
deal coffin for the common man.
How many golden coffins can anyone want?

Of those who appear at the alley-end,
they prefer the advance buyers. It takes know-how
to select a coffin for yourself.
'In our family it's cancer. Allow for shrinkage.'
'Dropsy does us. Add it on to the width.'
Can a man know the shape of the wood
that will encase him? Can a woman
close her eyes and breathe in the scent of cedar?

These are the ones the coffin-makers like
to sit with by the spirit-lamp. For these they bring out
tea-plums, infuse *Silver Needle*
and drink before they do the measuring.
Time to compare wood-shavings,
rubbing their curls between the fingers. Meanwhile
man and wife from the flat upstairs
take their blue bird for a walk
to the evening park, still in its cage.

Inside out

Snug as a devil's toenail embedded
in blue liass, plastic
in your movements as in dreams, you kick
for headiness at the rich
red walls that close on you like elastic.

But now they've shucked you out, bare-naked
in the devil's kitchen, toes curled
flinching from chip scraps, ash,
lino sticky with beer tack,
the nail-on-nylon scrape of the cold world.

You are born, wed, dead, buried.
The wooden walls of your coffin
grip like hands, reassuring. You bang them
for joy that they'll bang back, booming
that you're hidden, hidden, hidden within.

The blessing

The halls are thronged, the grand staircase murmurous.
There's a smell of close-packed bodies, lilac,
hair-gel and sweat. Handprints on the brass railings
fade like breath on a cold window.
Outside the city is stunned with snow.

There he is, just where he should be
by that leather-topped, deeply-scored table
where fortunes are lost and made. He explains,
and those at the back lean closer
to catch the ripple of laughter.

A joke, and the group dissolves
to stare, study, and point a finger.
He waits for them to catch up with him.
You need a guide, with so many rooms
and between them, so many turnings.

I am there too, but not speaking.
I wait while the paint peels,
alone with the pulse of a Matisse
and the sunlight beating full on us.
But perhaps I say this

as I see him hasten down another staircase:
'You always had a blessing with you,
and you still have a blessing with you.
Keep moving. Go as fast as you can
and whatever I say, don't listen.'

ites to run
ool bus.

id caught it
as she wiped stars the window –
the frost mended its web
and she put her snow-cool hand to my forehead.

The baby peeked round her skirts
trying to make me laugh
but I said my head hurt
and shut my eyes on her and coughed.

My mother kneeled
until her shape hid the whole world.
She buffed up my pillows as she held me.
'Could you eat a lemon sole?' she asked me.

It was her favourite
she would buy it as a treat for us.
I only liked the sound of it
slim, holy and expensive

but I said 'Yes, I will eat it'
and I shut my eyes and sailed out
on the noise of sunlight, white sheets
and lemon sole softly being cut up.

Christmas caves

A draught like a bony finger
felt under the door

but my father swung the coal scuttle
till the red cave of the fire roared

and the pine-spiced Christmas tree
shook out plumage of glass and tinsel.

The radio was on but ignored,
greeting 'Children all around the world'

and our Co-op Christmas turkey
had gone astray in the postal system –

the headless, green-gibletted corpse
revolved in the sorting-room

its leftover flesh
never to be eaten.

Tomorrow's potatoes rolled to the boil
and a chorister sang like a star

glowing by the lonely moon –
but he was not so far,

though it sounded like Bethlehem
and I was alone in the room

with the gold-netted sherry bottle
and wet black walnuts in a jar.

That violet-haired lady

That violet-haired lady, dowager-
humped, giving herself so many
smiles, taut glittering smiles,
smiles that swallow the air in front of her,
smiles that cling to shop-mirrors
and mar their silvering, smiles
like a spider's wrinklework
flagged over wasteland bushes –

she's had so many nips and tucks,
so much mouse-delicate
invisible mending. Her youth
squeaks out of its prison –
the dark red bar of her mouth
opening and closing.
She wants her hair to look black,
pure black, so she strands it with violet,
copperleaf, burgundy, rust –
that violet-haired lady, dowager-
humped, giving herself
so many smiles, keeping the light on.

Whooper swans

They fly
        straight-necked and barely white
            above the bruised stitching of clouds
              above wind and the sound of storms
            above the creak of the tundra
             the howl of weather
               the scatter
                 and wolfish gloom
                    of sleet icing their wings,

they come

      on their strong-sheathed wings
        looking at nothing
          straight down a freezing current of light,
          they might
            astonish a sleepy pilot
              tunnelling his route above the Arctic,

      his instruments darken and wink
        circling the swans
        and through his dull high window at sunrise
          he sees them
            ski their freezing current of light
              at twenty-seven thousand feet
                past grey-barrelled engines
                  spitting out heat
                    across the flight of the swans,

and they're gone
              the polar current sleeking them down
              as soon as he sees them.

Snow Queen

Long long I have looked for you,
snowshoeing across the world
across the wild white world

with my heart in my pocket
and my black-greased boots
to keep the cold out,

past cathedrals and pike marshes
I've tracked you,
so long I have looked for you.

In your star-blue palace
I wandered and could not find you
in your winter garden
I picked icicles,

my fingers burned on your gate
of freezing iron
I have the pain
of it yet on my palm,

through clanging branches
and black frost-fall
I dared not call

so I slide above worlds of ice
where the fishes kiss

and the drowned farmer
whips on his cart
through bubbles of glass

and his dogs prance
at the tail-end, frozen
with one leg cocked
and their yellow urine

twined in thickets of ice.
I stamp my boot
and the ice booms.

I have looked so long
I am wild and white
as your creatures, I might
be one of your own.

The cuckoo game

It starts with breaking into the wood
through a wave of chestnut leaves.

I am grey as a spring morning
fat and fuzzy as pussy willow,

all around I feel them simmering
those nests I've laid in,

like burst buds, a hurt place
lined for the young who've gone

unfledged to the ground.
There they splay, half-eaten

and their parents see nothing
but the one that stays.

This is the weather that cuckoos love:
the breaking of buds,

I am grey in the woods, burgling
the body-heat of birds,

riding the surf of chestnut flowers
on spread feathers.

I love the kiss of a carefully-built nest
in my second of pausing –

this is the way we grow
we cuckoos,

if you think cuckoos never come back
we do. We do.

The butcher's daughter

Where have you been, my little daughter
out in the wild weather?

I have met with a sailor, mother,
he has given me five clubs for juggling
and says I must go with him for ever.

Oh no, my treasure
you must come in and stay for ever
for you are the butcher's daughter.

Where have you been, my little daughter
in the winter weather?

I have met a man of war, mother,
he has given me four hoops to dance through
and he says I must love him for ever.

Oh no, my treasure
you must come in and shut the door
for you are the butcher's daughter.

Where have you been, my little daughter,
out in stormy weather?

I have met with a prince, mother,
he has given me three promises
and I must rule his heart for ever.

Oh no, my treasure
you must give back his promises
for you are the butcher's daughter.

Where have you been, my little daughter
in the wild of the weather?

I have spoken to a wise man, mother,
who gave me knowledge of good and evil
and said I must learn from him for ever.

Oh no, my treasure
you have no need of his knowledge
for you are the butcher's daughter.

Where have you been, my little, daughter
out in the summer weather?

I have met with a butcher, mother,
and he is sharpening a knife for me
for I am the butcher's daughter.

The greenfield ghost

The greenfield ghost is not much of a ghost,
it is a ghost of dammed-up streams,
it is a ghost of slow walks home
and sunburn and blackberry stains.

The greenfield ghost is not much of a ghost.
It is the ghost of low-grade land,
it is the ghost of lovers holding hands
on evening strolls out of town.

The greenfield ghost is not much of a ghost.
It is the ghost of mothers at dusk calling,
it is the ghost of children leaving their dens
for safe houses which will cover them.

Herring girl

See this 'un here, this little bone needle,
he belonged to the net menders.

I heard the crackle in your throat
like fishbone caught there, not words.

And this other 'un, he's wood, look,
you said to the radio interviewer

and I couldn't see the fine-fashioned needle
or the seams on your face,

but I heard the enormous hiss of herring
when they let the tailboard down

and the buyers bargaining
as the tide reached their boots,

I heard the heave of the cart, the herring girls'
laugh as they flashed their knives –

Such lovely voices we all had
you ought t' have heard us
singing like Gracie Fields
or else out of the hymn book.

Up to your elbows, you gutted
your pile of herring. The sludge

was silver, got everywhere.
Your hands were fiery and blooded.

from the slash and the tweak and the salt
and the heap of innards for the gulls.

I'd put a little bit o' bandage round these fingers
– you can see where they been nicked,

we had to keep going so quick
we could never wear gloves.

Russian doll

When I held you up to my cheek you were cold
when I came close to your smile it dissolved,

the paint on your lips was as deep
as the steaming ruby of beetroot soup

but your breath smelled of varnish and pine
and your eyes swivelled away from mine.

When I wanted to open you up
you glowed, dumpy and perfect

smoothing your dozen little selves
like rolls of fat under your apron

and I hadn't the heart to look at them.
I knew I would be spoiling something.

But when I listened to your heart
I heard the worlds inside of you spinning
like the earth on its axis spinning.

Breeze of ghosts

Tall ship hanging out at the horizon
tall ship blistering the horizon
you've been there so long
your sheets and decks white
in the sun

what wind whispers you in?

Tall ship creaking at the horizon
your captain long gone
your crew in the cabin
drinking white rum
their breath spiralling

what wind breathes you in?

Tall ship tilting to the shoreline
past Spanish palms
tall ship coming in like a swan
in the midday sun

what wind blows you in?

It is the cool
wind of the morning
stirring my masts
before the sun
burns it to nothing,
they call it
breeze of ghosts.

THE APPLE FALL

The marshalling yard

In the goods yard the tracks are unmarked.
Snow lies, the sky is full of it.
Its hush swells in the dark.

Grasped by black ice on black
a massive noise of breathing
fills the tracks;

cold women, ready for departure
smooth their worn skirts
and ice steals through their hands like children
from whose touch they have already been parted.

Now like a summer
the train comes
beating the platform
with its blue wings.

The women stir. They sigh.
Feet slide
warm on a wooden stairway
then a voice calls and
milk drenched with aniseed
drawls on the walk to school.

At last they leave.
Their breathless neighbours
steal from the woods, the barns,
and tender straw
sticks to their palms.

A cow here in the June meadow

A cow here in the June meadow
where clouds pile, tower above tower.

We lie, buried in sunburn,
our picnic a warm
paper of street tastes,

she like a gold cloud
steps, moony.
Her silky rump dips
into the grasses, buffeting
a mass of seed ready to run off in flower.

We stroll under the elder, smell
wine, trace blackfly along its leaf-veins

then burning and yawning we pile
kisses onto the hot upholstery.

Now evening shivers along the water surface.
The cow, suddenly planted stands – her tender
skin pollened all over –
ready to nudge all night at the cold grasses,
her udder heavily and more heavily swinging.

Zelda

At Great Neck one Easter
were Scott
Ring Lardner
and Zelda, who sat
neck high in catalogues like reading cards

her hair in curl for
wild stories, applauded.
A drink, two drinks and a kiss.

Scott and Ring both love her –
gold-headed, sky-high Miss
Alabama. (The lioness
with still eyes and no affectations
doesn't come into this.)

Some visitors said she ought
to do more housework, get herself taught
to cook.
Above all, find some silent occupation
rather than mess up Scott's vocation.

In France her barriers were simplified.
Her husband developed a work ethic:
film actresses; puritan elegance;

tipped eyes spilling material
like fresh Americas. You see
said Scott   they know about work, like me.

You can't beat a writer for justifying adultery.

Zelda
always wanted to be a dancer

she said, writhing
among the gentians that smelled of medicine.

A dancer in a sweat lather is not beautiful.
A dancer's mind can get fixed.

Give me a wooden floor, a practice dress,
a sheet of mirrors and hours of labour

and lie me with my spine to the floor
supple   secure.

She handed these back too
with her gold head and her senses.

She asks for visits. She makes herself hollow
with tears, dropped in the same cup.
Here at the edge of her sensations
there is no chance.

Evening falls on her Montgomery verandah.
No cars come by. Her only visitor
his voice, slender along the telephone wire.

The Polish husband

The traffic halted
and for a moment
the broad green avenue
hung like a wave

while a woman crossing
stopped me and said

'Can you show me my wedding?
– In which church is it going to be held?'

The lorries hooted at her
as she stood there on the island
for her cloak fell back
and under it her legs were bare.
Her hair was dyed blonde
and her sad face deeply tanned.

I asked her 'What is the name of your husband?'
She wasn't sure, but she knew his first name was Joe,
she'd met him in Poland
and this was the time for the wedding.

There was a cathedral behind us
and a sign to the centre of the town.
'I am not an expert on weddings,'
I said, 'but take that honey-coloured building
which squats on its lawns like a cat –
at least there's music playing inside it.'

So she ran with her heels tapping
and the long, narrow folds of her cloak falling apart.
A veil on wire flew from her head,
her white figure ducked in the porch and blew out.

But Joe, the Polish man. In the rush of this town
I can't say whether she even found him
to go up the incense-heavy church beside him
under the bridal weight of her clothes,
or whether he was one of the lorry drivers
to whom her brown, hurrying legs were exposed.

The damson

Where have you gone
small child,
the damson bloom
on your eyes

the still heap
of your flesh
lightly composed
in a grey shawl,

your skull's pulse
stains you,
the veins slip deep.

Two lights burn
at the mouth of the cave
where the air's thin
and the tunnels boom
with your slippery blood.

Your unripe cheeks cling
to the leaves, to the wall,
your grasp unpeels
and your bruises murmur

while blueness clouds
on the down of your eyes,
your tears erode
and your smile files

through your lips like a soldier
who shoots at the sky
and you flash up in silver;

where are you now
little one,
peeled almond,
damson bloom?

In Rodmell Garden

It's past nine and breakfast is over.
With morning frost on my hands I cross
the white grass, and go nowhere.

It's icy: domestic. A grain
of coffee burns my tongue. Its heat
folds into the first cigarette.

The garden and air are still.
I am a stone and the world falls from me.

I feet untouchable – a new planet
where life knows it isn't safe to begin.
From silver flakes of ash I shape
a fin and watch it with anguish.

I hear apples rolling above me;
November twigs; a bare existence –

my sister is a marvellous
dolphin, flanking her young.
Her blood flushes her skin

but mine is trapped. Occasional moments
allow me to bathe in their dumb sweetness.

My loose pips ripen. My night subsides
rushing, like the long glide of an owl.

Raw peace. A pale, frost-lit morning.
The black treads of my husband on the lawn
as he goes from the house to the loft
                        laying out apples.

The apple fall

In a back garden I'm painting
the outside toilet in shell and antelope.
The big domestic bramley tree
hangs close to me, rosy and leafless.
Sometimes an apple thumps
into the bushes I've spattered with turpentine
while my brush moves with a suck
over the burnt-off door frame.

Towels from the massage parlour
are out on the line next door:
all those bodies sweating into them
each day – the fabric stiffening –
towels bodiless and sex over.

I load the brush with paint again
and I hear myself breathing.
Sun slips off the wall
so the yard is cool
and lumbered with shadows,

and then a cannonade of apples
punches the wall and my arms,
the ripe stripes on their cheeks fall open,
flesh spurts and the juices fizz and glisten.

Pharaoh's daughter

The slowly moving river in summer
where bulrushes, nallow and water forget-me-not
slip to their still faces.

A child's body
joins their reflections,

his plastic boat
drifts into midstream
and though I lean down to
brown water that smells of peppermint
I can't get at it:
my willow branch flails and pushes the boat outwards.

He smiles quickly
and tells me it doesn't matter;
my feet grip in the mud
and mash blue flowers under them.

Then we go home
masking with summer days the misery
that has haunted a whole summer.

I think once of the Egyptian woman
who drew a baby from the bulrushes
hearing it mew in the damp
odrorous growth holding its cradle.

There's nothing here but the boat
caught by its string
and through this shimmering day I struggle
drawn down by the webbed
years, the child's life cradled within.

Domestic poem

So, how decisive a house is:
quilted, a net of blood and green
droops on repeated actions at nightfall.

A bath run through the wall
comforts the older boy sleeping
meshed in the odours of breath and Calpol

while in the maternity hospital
ancillaries rinse out the blood bottles;

the feel and the spore
of babies' sleep stays here.

Later, some flat-packed plastic
swells to a parachute of oxygen
holding the sick through their downspin,

now I am well enough, I
iron, and place the folded sheets in bags
from which I shall take them, identical,
after the birth of my child.

And now the house closes us,
                        close on us,
like fruit we rest in its warm branches

and though it's time for the child to come
nobody knows it, the night passes

while I sleepwalk the summer heat.

Months shunt me and I bring you
like an old engine hauling the blue
spaces that flash between track and train time.

Mist rises, smelling of petrol's
burnt offerings, new born,

oily and huge, the lorries drum
on Stokes' Croft,

out of the bathroom mirror the sky
is blue and pale as a Chinese mountain.

and I breathe in.

It's time to go now. I take nothing
but breath, thinned.
A blown-out dandelion globe
might choose my laundered body to grow in.

Patrick I

Patrick, I cannot write
such poems for you as a father might
coming upon your smile,

your mouth half sucking, half sleeping,
your tears shaken from your eyes like sparklers
break up the nightless weeks of your life:

lighthearted, I go to the kitchen
and cook breakfast, aching as you grow hungry.
Mornings are plain as the pages
of books in sedentary schooldays.

If I were eighty and lived next door
hanging my pale chemises on the porch
would I envy or pity my neighbour?

Polished and still as driftwood
she stands smoothing her dahlias;

liquid, leaking,
I cup the baby's head to my shoulder:

the child's a boy and will not share
one day these obstinate, exhausted mornings.

Patrick II

The other babies were more bitter than you
Patrick, with your rare, tentative cry,
your hours of steep, snuffing the medical air.

Give me time for your contours, your fierce drinking.
Like land that has been parched for half a summer
and smiles, sticky with feeding

I have examined and examined you
at midnight, at two days; I have accompanied you
to the blue world on another floor of the hospital
where half-formed babies open their legs like anemones
and nurses, specialised as astronauts,
operate around the apnoea pillows.

But here you bloomed. You survived,
sticky with nectar. X-rayed, clarified,
you came back, dirty and peaceful.

And now like sunflowers settling their petals
for the last strokes of light in September
your eyes turn to me at 3 a.m.

You meet my stiff, mucousy face
and snort, beating your hand on my breast
as one more feed flows through the darkness, timed
to nothing now but the pull of your mouth.

Weaning

Cool as sleep, the crates ring.
Birds stir and my milk stings me;
you slip my grasp. I never find you
in dreams – only your mouth
not crying
your sleep still pressing on mine.

The carpets shush. The house back silences.
I turn with you, wide-lipped
blue figure

into the underground of babies
and damp mothers fumbling at bras

and the first callus grows on us
weaned from your night smiles.

Approaches to winter

Now I write off a winter of growth.
First, hands batting the air,
forehead still smeared,

– now, suddenly, he stands there
upright and rounded as a tulip.
The garden sparkles through the windows.

Dark and a heap in my arms;
the thermostat clicking all night.
Out in the road beached cars and winter
so cold five minutes would finish you.

Light fell in its pools
each evening. Tranquilly
it stamped the same circles.

Friends shifted their boots on the step.
Their faces gleamed from their scarves
that the withdrawal of day
brought safety.

Experience so stitched, intimate,
mutes me.
Now I'm desperate for solitude.
The house enrages me.

I go miles, pushing the pram,
thinking about Christina Rossetti's
black dresses – my own absent poems.

I go miles, touching his blankets proudly,
drawing the quilt to his lips.

I write of winter and the approaches to winter.
Air clings to me, rotten Lord Derbies,
patched in their skins, thud down.
The petals of Michaelmas daisies give light.

Now I'm that glimpsed figure for children
occupying doorways and windows;
that breath of succulence
ignored till nightfall.

I go out before the curtains are drawn
and walk close to the windows
which shine secretly.
Bare to the street
red pleats of a lampshade expose
bodies in classic postures, arguing.

Their senseless jokes explode with saliva.
I mop and tousle.

It's three o'clock in the cul-de-sac.
Out of the reach of traffic,
free from the ply
of bodies glancing and crossing,
the shopping, visiting,
cashing orders at the post office,

I lie on my bed in the sun
drawing down streams of babble.
This room holds me, a dull
round bulb stubbornly
rising year after year in the same place.

The night chemist

In the chemist's at night-time
swathed counters and lights turned down
lean and surround us.

Waiting for our prescriptions
we clock these sounds:
a baby's peaked hush,
hawked breath.

I pay a pound
and pills fall in my curled palms.
Holding their white packages tenderly
patients track back to the pain.

'Why is the man shouting?' Oliver asks me.
I answer, 'He wants to go home.'
Softly, muffled by cloth
the words still come
and the red-streaked drunkard goes past us,
rage scalding us.

I would not dare bring happiness
into the chemist's at night-time.
Its gift-wrapped lack of assistance still presses
as suffering closes the blinded windows.

St Paul's

This evening clouds darken the street quickly,
more and more grey
flows throngh the yellowing treetops,

traffic flies downhill
roaring and spangled with faces,
full buses
rock past the Sussex Place roundabout.

In Sussex the line of Downs
has no trees to uncover,
no lick of the town's wealth, blue
in smoke, no gold, fugitive dropping.
In villages old England
checks rainfall, sick of itself.

Here there are scraps and flashes:
bellying food smells – last-minute buying –
plantain, quarters of ham.
The bread shop lady pulls down
loaves that will make tomorrow's cheap line.

On offer are toothpaste and shoe soles
mended same day for Monday's interview
and a precise network of choices
for old women collecting their pension
on Thursday, already owing the rent man.

Some places are boarded. You lose your expectancy –
soon it appears you never get home. Still
it's fine on evenings and in October
to settle here. Still the lights splashing look beautiful.

Poem for December 28

My nephews with almond faces
black hair like bunces of grapes

    (the skin stroked and then bruised
    the head buried and caressed)

he takes his son's head in his hands
kisses it   blesses it   leaves it:

the boy with circles under his eyes like damsons
not the blond baby, the stepson.

In the forest stories about the black
father   the jew   the incubus

if there are more curses they fall on us.

Behind the swinging ropes of their isolation
my nephews wait, sucking their sweets.
The hall fills quickly and neatly.

If they keep still as water
   I'll know them.
I look but I can't be certain:

my nephews with heavy eyelids
blowing in the last touches of daylight

my sisters raising them up like torches.

Greenham Common

Today is barred with darkness of winter.
In cold tents women protest,
for once unveiled, eyes stinging with smoke.

They stamp round fires in quilted anoraks,
glamourless, they laugh often
and teach themselves to speak eloquently.
Mud and the camp's raw bones
set them before the television camera.

Absent, the women of old photographs
holding the last of their four children,
eyes darkened, hair covered,
bodies waxy as cyclamen;
absent, all these suffering ones.

New voices rip at the throat,
new costumes, metamorphoses.

Soft-skirted, evasive
women were drawn from the ruins,
swirls of ash on them like veils.

History came as a seducer
and said: this is the beauty of women
in bombfall. Dolorous
you curl your skirts over your sleeping children.

Instead they stay at this place
all winter; eat from packets and jars,
keep sensible, don't hunger,
battle each day at the wires.

Poem for hidden women

'Fuck this staring paper and table –
I've just about had enough of it.

I'm going out for some air,'
he says, letting the wind bang up his sheets of poems.

He walks quickly; it's cool,
and rainy sky covers both stars and moon.
Out of the windows come slight
echoes of conversations receding upstairs.

There. He slows down.
A dark side–street – thick bushes –
he doesn't see them.
He smokes. Leaves can stir as they please.

(We clack like jackrabbits from pool to pool of lamplight.
Stretching our lips, we walk exposed
as milk cattle past heaps of rubbish

killed by the edge
of knowledge that trees hide
a face slowly detaching itself
from shadow, and starting to smile.)

The poet goes into the steep alleys
close to the sea, where fish scales line the gutter
and women prostitute themselves to men
as men have described in many poems.

They've said how milky, or bitter
as lemons they find her –
the smell of her hair
...vanilla...cinnamon...
there's a smell for every complexion.

Cavafy tells us he went always
to secret rooms and purer vices;
he wished to dissociate himself
from the hasty unlacings of citizens
fumbling, capsizing –
white
flesh in a mound and kept from sight,

but he doesn't tell us
whether these boys' hair always smelled of cinnamon
or if their nights cost more than spices.

A woman goes into the night café,
chooses a clean
knife and a spoon
and takes up her tray.
Quickly the manageress leans from the counter.
(As when a policeman arrests a friend
her eyes plunge and her voice roughens.)
She points to a notice with her red nail:
'After 11 we serve only accompanied females.'

The woman fumbles her grip
on her bag, and it slips.
Her forces tumble.
People look on as she scrabbles
for money and tampax.
A thousand shadows accompany her
down the stiff lino, through the street lighting.

The poet sits in a harbour bar
where the tables are smooth and solid to lean on.
It's peaceful. Men gaze
for hours at beer and brass glistening.
The sea laps. The door swings.

The poet feels poems
invade him. All day he has been stone-breaking
he says. He would be happier in cafés
in other countries, drinking, watching;

he feels he's a familiar sort of poet
but he's at ease with it.
Besides, he's not actually writing a poem:
there's plenty, he's sure,
in drink and hearing the sea move.

For what is Emily Dickinson doing
back at the house – the home?
A doctor emerges, wiping his face,
and pins a notice on the porch.
After a while you don't even ask.

No history
gets at this picture:
a woman named Sappho
sat in bars by purple water
with her feet crossed at the ankles
and her hair flaming with violets
never smiling when she didn't feel like it.

'End here, it's hopeful,'
says the poet, getting up from the table.

If no revolution come

If no revolution come
star clusters
will brush heavy on the sky

and grapes burst
into the mouths of fifteen
well-fed men,

these honest men
will build them houses like pork palaces
if no revolution come,

short-life dust children
will be crumbling in the sun –
they have to score like this
if no revolution come.

The sadness of people
don't look at it too long:
you're studying for madness
if no revolution come.

If no revolution come
it will be born sleeping,
it will be heavy as baby
playing on mama's bones,

it will be gun-thumping on Sunday
and easy good time
for men who make money,

for men who make money
grow like a roof
so the rubbish of people
can't live underneath.

If no revolution come
star clusters
will drop heavy from the sky

and blood burst
out of the mouths of fifteen
washing women,

and the land-owners will drink us
one body by one:
they have to score like this
if no revolution come.

A safe light

I hung up the sheets in moonlight,
surprised that it really was so
steady, a quickly moving pencil

flowing onto the stained cotton.
How the valves
in that map
of taut fabric
blew in and blew out

then spread flat
over the tiles
while the moon filled them with light.

A hundred feet above the town
for once the moonscape showed nothing extraordinary

only the clicking pegs
and radio news from our kitchen.
One moth hesitated
tapping at our lighted window

and in the same way the moonlight
covered the streets, all night.

Near Dawlish

Her fast asleep face turns from me,
the oil on her eyelids gleams
and the shadow of a removed moustache
darkens the curve of her mouth,

her lips are still flattened together
and years occupy her face,
her holiday embroidery glistens,
her fingers quiver then rest.

I perch in my pink dress
sleepiness fanning my cheeks,
not lurching, not touching
as the train leaps.

Mother you should not be sleeping.
Look how dirty my face is, and lick
the smuts off me with your salt spit.

Golden corn rocks to the window
as the train jerks. Your narrowing body leaves me
frightened, too frightened to cry for you.

The last day of the exhausted month

The last day of the exhausted month
of August. Hydrangeas
purple and white like flesh immersed in water
with no shine
to keep the air off them
open their tepid petals more and more widely.

The newly-poured tar smells antiseptic
like sheets moulding on feverish skin:
surfaces of bedrock, glasslike passivity.

The last day of the exhausted month
goes quickly. A brown parcel
arrives with clothes left at the summer lodgings,
split and too small.
A dog noses
better not look at it too closely
God knows why they bothered to send them at all.

A smell of cat
joins us just before eating.

The cat is dead but its brown
smell still seeps from my tub of roses.

The deserted table

Coiled peel goes soft on the deserted table
where faïence, bubble glasses, and the rest
of riches thicken.

People have left their bread and potatoes.
Each evening baskets
of broken dinner hit the disposal unit.

Four children, product of two marriages,
two wives, countless slighter relations
and friends all come to the table

bringing new wines discovered on holiday,
fresh thirtyish faces, the chopped
Japanese dip of perfectly nourished hairstyles,
more children, more confident voices,
wave after wave consuming the table.

The writer's son

The father is a writer; the son
(almost incapable of speech)
explores him.

'Why did you take my language
my childhood
my body all sand?

why did you gather my movements
waves pouncing
eyes steering me till I crumbled?

We're riveted. I'm in the house
hung up with verbiage like nets.
A patchwork monster at the desk
bending the keys of your electric typewriter.

You're best at talking. I know
your hesitant, plain vowels.
Your boy's voice, blurred,
passed through my cot bars, stealing my baby magic.
You were the one they smiled at.'

Ollie and Charles at St Andrew's Park

Up at the park once more
the afternoon ends.
My sister and I huddle in quilted jackets.

A cigarette burn
crinkles the pushchair waterproofs,
the baby relaxes
sucking his hood's curled edges.

Still out of breath
from shoving and easing the wheels
on broken pavement we stay here.
Daffodils break in the wintry bushes

and Ollie and Charles in drab parkas
run, letting us wait by the swings.
Under eskimo hoods their hair springs
dun coloured, child-smelling.

They squat, and we speak quietly,
occasionally scanning the indigo patched
shadows with children melted against them.

Winter fairs

The winter fairs are all over.
The smells of coffee and naphtha
thin and are quite gone.

An orange tossed in the air
hung like a wonder
everyone would catch once,

the children's excitable cheeks
and woollen caps that they wore
tight, up to the ears,
are all quietened, disbudded;

now am I walking the streets
noting a bit of gold paper? –
a curl of peel suggesting the whole
aromatic globe in the air.

In a wood near Turku

The summer cabins are padlocked.
Their smell of sandshoes
evaporates over the lake water
leaving pine walls to shoulder the ice.

Resin seals them in hard splashes.
The woodman
knocks at their sapless branches.

He gets sweet puffballs
and chanterelles in his jacket,
strips off fungus like yellow leather,
thumbs it, then hacks the tree trunk.

Hazy and cold as summer dawn
the day goes on,

wood rustles on wood,
close, as the mist thins
like smoke around the top of the pine trees
and once more the saw whines.

Landscape from the Monet Exhibition at Cardiff

My train halts in the snowfilled station.
Gauges tick and then cease
on ice as the track settles
and iron-bound rolling stock creaks.

Two work-people
walk up alongside us,
wool-wadded, shifting their picks,

the sun, small as a rose,
buds there in the distance.
The gangs throw handfuls of salt like sowers
and light fires to keep the points moving.

Here are trees, made with two strokes.
A lady with a tray of white teacups
walks lifting steam from window to window.

I'd like to pull down the sash and stay
here in the blue where it's still work time.
The hills smell cold and are far away
at standstill, where lamps bloom.

Breakfast

Often when the bread tin is empty
and there's no more money for the fire
I think of you, and the breakfast you laid for me
– black bread and honey and beer.

I threw out a panful of wine yesterday –
the aluminium had turned sour –
I have two colours of bread to choose from,
I'd take the white if I were poor,

so indigence is distant as my hands
stiff in unheated washing water,
but you, with your generous gift of butter
and cheese with poppy seeds, all in one morning meal

have drawn the blinds up at the bedside window
and I can watch the ships' tall masts appear.

FROM

THE SEA SKATER

(1986)

The bride's nights in a strange village

At three in the morning
while mist limps between houses
while cloaks and blankets
dampen with dew

the bride sleeps with her husband
bundled in a red blanket,
her mouth parts and a bubble
of sour breathing goes free.
She humps wool up to her ears
while her husband tightens his arms
and rocks her, mumbling. Neither awakes.

In the second month of the marriage
the bride wakes after midnight.
Damp-bodied
she lunges from sleep
hair pricking with sweat
breath knocking her sides.
She eels from her husband's grip
and crouches, listening.

The night is enlarged by sounds.
The rain has started.
It threshes leaves secretively
and there in the blackness
of whining dogs it finds out the house.
Its hiss enfolds her, blots up
her skin, then sifts off, whispering
in her like mirrors
the length of the rainy village.

Christmas roses

I remember years ago, that we had Christmas roses:
cold, greeny things under the snow –
fantastic hellebores, harbingers
of the century's worst winter.

On little fields stitched over with drystone
we broke snow curds, our sledge
tossing us out at the wall.

For twelve years a plateau of sea
stopped at my parents' window.
Here the slow Flatholm foghorn
sucking at the house fabric

recalls my little month-old brother,
kept in the house for weeks
while those snow days piled up like plates
to an impossible tower.

They were building the match factory
to serve moors seeded with conifers
that year of the Bay of Pigs,

the year of Cuba, when adults muttered
of taking to the moors with a shotgun
when the bomb dropped.

Such conversation, rapaciously
stored in a nine-year-old's memory
breeds when I stare down Bridgwater Bay
to that glassy CEGB elegance, Hinkley
Point, treating the landscape like snow,
melting down marshes and long, lost
muddy horizons.

Fir thickets replace those cushions
of scratchy heather, and prick out the noise
of larks in the air, so constant
I never knew what it was.

Little hellebores with green veins,
not at all tender, and scentless
on frosty ground, with your own small
melt, your engine of growth:
that was the way I liked you.

I imagine you sent back from Africa

I imagine you sent back from Africa
leaving a patchwork of rust and khaki
sand silt in your tea and your blood.

The metal of tanks and cans
puckers your taste-buds.
Your tongue jumps from the touch
of charge left in a dying battery.

You spread your cards in the shade
of roving lorries whose canvas
tents twenty soldiers.
The greased cards patter
in chosen spaces.

I imagine you sent back from Africa
with a tin mug kept for the bullet hole
in at one angle and out another.

You mount the train at the port
asking if anywhere on earth
offers such grey, mild people.

Someone draws down the blind.
You see his buttons, his wrist,
his teeth filled to the roots.
He weakens the sunlight for you
and keeps watch on your face.
Your day sinks in a hollow of sleep
racket and megaphoned voices.

The troop-ship booms once. Laden
with new men she moves down the Sound
low in the water, egg-carrying.

But for you daylight
with your relieved breath
supping up train dirt.
A jolt is a rescue from sleep
and a glaze of filth from the arm-rest
patches your cheek. You try to catch voices
calling out stations closer to home.

In memoriam Cyril Smith 1913-1945

I've approached him since childhood,
since he was old, blurred,

my stake in the playground chants
and war games,

a word like 'brother'
mixed with a death story.

Wearing shorts and a smile
he stayed in the photograph box.

His hair was receding early.
He had Grandpa's long lip and my mother's love.

The jungle obliterates a city
of cries and murmurs,
bloody discharges
and unsent telegrams.

Now he is immanent

breaking off thoughts

printing that roll of film
one sweaty evening,

Four decades
have raised a thicket of deaths around him

a fence of thorn and a fence of roses.

His mother, my grandmother,
his father, his brother,

his camp companions

his one postcard.

The circle closes
in skin, limbs
and new resemblances.

We wanted to bring him
through life with us

but he grows younger.

We've passed him
holding out arms.

The parachute packers

The parachute packers with white faces
swathed over with sleep
and the stale bodily smell of sheets

make haste to tin huts where a twelve-hour
shift starts in ten minutes.
Their bare legs pump bicycle pedals,
they clatter on wooden-soled sandals
into the dazzling light over the work benches.

They rub in today's issue of hand-cream.
Their fingers skim on the silk
as the unwieldy billows of parachute flatten
like sea-waves, oiled, folded in sevens.

The only silk to be had
comes in a military packaging:
dull-green, printed, discreet,
gone into fashioning parachutes
to be wondered at like the flowers'
down-spinning, seed-bearing canopies
lodged in the silt of village memory.

A girl pulling swedes in a field
senses the shadow of parachutes
and gapes up, knees braced
and hair tangling. She must be riddled,
her warm juices all spilled
for looking upwards too early
into the dawn, leafy with parachutes.

Heavenly wide canopies
bring down stolid chaps with their rifle butts
ready to crack, with papers
to govern the upturned land,
with boots, barbed wire and lists on fine paper
thousands of names long.

I look up now at two seagulls,
at cloud drifts and a lamp-post
bent like a feeding swan,

and at the sound of needles
seaming up parachutes in Nissen huts
with a hiss and pull through the stuff
of these celestial ball-dresses

for nuns, agents, snow-on-the-boots men
sewn into a flower's corolla
to the music of *Workers' Playtime*.

At dusk the parachute packers
release their hair from its nets
and ride down lanes whitened by cow-parsley
to village halls, where the dances
and beer and the first cigarettes
expunge the clouds of parachute silk
and rules touching their hair and flesh.

In the bar they're the girls who pack parachutes
for our boys. They can forget
the coughs of the guard on duty,
the boredom and long hours
and half-heard cries of caught parachutists.

Porpoise washed up on the beach

After midday the great lazy
slaps of the sea,
the whistling of a boy who likes the empty
hour while the beach is feeding,

the cliffs vacant, gulls untidily drowsing
far out on the water.

I walked on in the dazzle
round to the next cove
where the sea was running backwards like mercury
from people busy at cutting
windows in the side of a beached porpoise.

The creature had died recently.
Naturally its blood was mammalian,
its skin supple and tough; it made me
instantly think of uses for it –
shoe soling, sealing the hulls of boats –
something to explain the intent knives
and people swiftly looking at me.

But there was no mussel harvest on the rocks
or boat blinding through noon
out to the crab pots,
not here but elsewhere the settled
stupor of digestion went on.

The porpoise had brought the boys between fourteen and eighteen,
lengthened their lives by a burning
profitless noon-time,
so they cut windows out of surprise
or idleness, finding the thing here
like a blank wall, inviting them.

They jumped from its body, prodded it,
looked in its mouth and its eyes,
hauled up its tail like a child's drawing
and became serious.

Each had the use of the knife in turn
and paused over the usual graffiti
to test words first with a knife-point
and fit the grey boulder of flesh under them.

Clapping their wings the gulls came back from the sea,
the pink screens of the hotel opened,
the last boy scoured the knife with sand.

I walked back along the shingle
breathing away the bloody trail of the porpoise
and saw the boys' wet heads glittering,
their hooting, diving
bodies sweeping them out of the bay.

In deep water

For three years I've been wary of deep water.
I busied myself on the shore
towelling, handing out underwear
wading the baby knee-high.

I didn't think I had forgotten
how to play in the deep water,
but it was only today I went there
passing the paddle boats and bathers,
the parallel harbour wall,
until there was no one at all but me
rolling through the cold water
and scarcely bothering to swim
from pure buoyancy.

Of course I could still see them:
the red and the orange armbands,
the man smiling and pointing seawards,
the tender faces.

It's these faces that have taken me
out of the deep water
and made my face clench like my mother's
once, as I pranced on a ten-foot
wall over a glass-house.

The water remembers my body,
stretched and paler as it is.
Down there is my old reflection
spread-eagled, steadily moving.

Lady Macduff and the primroses

Now the snowdrop, the wood-anemone, the crocus
have flowered
and faded back to dry, scarcely-seen threads,

Lady Macduff goes down to the meadow
where primrose flowers are thickening.

Her maid told her this morning, It's time
to pick them now, there will never be more
without some dying.

Even the kitchen girls, spared for an hour,
come to pick flowers for wine.

The children's nurse has never seemed to grasp
that she only need lay down the flowers loosely,

the flat-bottomed baskets soon fill
with yellow, chill primroses covered by sturdy leaves,

but the nurse will weave posies
even though the children are impatient
and only care who is first, has most
of their mother's quick smile.

Pasties have been brought from the castle.
Savoury juices spill from their ornate crusts,
white cloths are smeared with venison gravy
and all eat hungrily
out in the spring wind.

Lady Macduff looks round at the sparkling
sharpness of grass, whipped kerchiefs and castle battlements
edged with green light

and the primroses like a fall
colder than rain, warmer than snow,
petals quite still, hairy stems helplessly curling.

She thinks how they will be drunk
as yellow wine, swallow by swallow
filling the pauses of mid-winter,
sweet to raw throats.

Mary Shelley

No living poet ever arrived at the fulness of his fame;
the jury which sits in judgement upon a poet, belonging
as he does to all time, must be composed of his peers.

PERCY BYSSHE SHELLEY

In the weightlessness of time and our passage within it
voices and rooms swim.
Cleft after soft cleft
parts, word-covered lips
thin as they speak.

I should recall how pink and tender
your lids looked when you read too long
while I produced seamed
patchwork, my own phantom.

Am I the jury, the evidence,
the recollection?

Last night I dreamed of a prospect
and so I dreamed backwards:

first I woke in the dark
scraping my knuckles on board and mould.

I remember half listening
or reading in the shadow of a fire;
each evening I would lie quietly
breathing the scent of my flesh till I slept.

I loved myself in my new dress.
I loved the coral stems rising from the rosebush
under my window in March.
I was intact, neat,
dressing myself each morning.

I dreamed my little baby was alive,
mewing for me from somewhere in the room.
I chafed her feet and tucked her nightdress close.

Claire, Shelley and I left England.
We crossed the Channel and boasted afterwards
of soaked clothes, vomit and cloudbursts.

We went by grey houses, shutters still closed,
people warmly asleep. My eyes were dazed
wide open in abatement and vacancy.

*

A bad wife is like winter in the house.
(diary of Claire Clairmont, Florence 1820)

In Florence in winter grit scoured between houses;
the plaster needed replacing, the children had coughs.

I lived in a nursery which smelled of boredom and liniment.
In bed I used to dream of water crossings
by night. I looked fixedly forward.
It was the first winter I became ugly:
I was unloving all winter,
frozen by my own omens.

In Lerici I watched small boats on the bay
trace their insect trails on the flat water.
Orange lamps and orange blossom
lit and suffused the night garden.

Canvas slashed in a squall.
Stifling tangles of sail and fragile
masts snapping brought the boat over.
The blackened sea
kept its waves still, then tilting
knocked you into its cold crevices.

I was pressed to a pinpoint,
my breath flat.
Scarcely pulsating
I gave out nothing.

I gave out nothing before your death.
We would pass in the house with blind-lipped
anger in me.
You put me aside for the winter.

I would soften like a season
I would moisten and turn to you.
I would not conform my arms to the shapes of dead children.

I patched my babies and fed them
but death got at them.
Your eyes fed everywhere.

I wonder at bodies once clustered,
at delicate tissue
emerging unable to ripen.

Each time I returned to life
calmer than the blood which left me
weightless as the ticking of a blind-cord.
Inside my amply-filled dress
I am renewed seamlessly.

Fledged in my widow's weeds
I was made over, for this
prickle of live flesh
wedged in its own corpulence.

The plum tree

The plum was my parents' tree,
above them
as I was at my bedroom window
wondering why they chose to walk this way quietly
under the plum tree.

My sisters and I stopped playing
as they reached up and felt for the fruit.
It lay among bunches of leaves,
oval and oozing resin
out into pearls of gum.
They bit into the plums
without once glancing
back at the house.

Some years were thin:
white mildew streaking the trunk,
fruit buckled and green,

but one April
the tree broke from its temperate blossoming
and by late summer the branches
trailed earth, heavy with pound
after pound of bursting Victorias,

and I remember the oblivious steps
my parents took as they went quietly
out of the house one summer evening
to stand under the plum tree.

The air-blue gown

Tonight I'm eating the past
consuming its traces,

the past is a heap
sparkling with razor blades
where patches of sweetness
deepen to compost,

woodlice fold up their legs
and roll luxuriously,

cold vegetation
rises to blood heat.

The local sea's bare
running up to the house

tufting its waves
with red seaweed
spread against a Hebridean noon.

Lightly as sandpipers marking the shoreline
boats at the jetty sprang
and rocked upon the green water.

Not much time passes, but suddenly
now when you're crumpled after a cold
I see how the scale and changes
of few words measure us.

At this time of year I remember a cuckoo's
erratic notes on a mild morning.
It lay full-fed on a cherry branch
repeating an hour of sweetness
its grey body unstirring
its lustrous eyes turning.

Talk sticks and patches
walls and the kitchen formica
while at the table outlines
seated on a thousand evenings
drain like light going out of a landscape.

The back door closes, swings shut,
drives me to place myself inside it.
In this flickering encampment
fire pours sideways
then once more stands
evenly burning.

I wake with a touch on my face
and turn sideways
butting my head into darkness.

The wind's banging diminishes. An aircraft
wanders through the upper atmosphere
bee-like, propelled by loneliness.
It searches for a fallen corolla,
its note rising and going
as it crosses the four quarters.

The city turns a seamed cheek upward,
confides itself to the sound and hazardous
construction of a journey by starlight.

I drop back soundlessly,
my lips slackened.
Headache alone is my navigator,
plummeting, shedding its petals.

It's Christmas Eve.
Against my nightdress a child's foot, burning,
passes its fever through the cotton,

the tide of bells swings
and the child winces.

The bells are shamelessly
clanging, the voices
hollering churchward.

I'm eating the past tonight
tasting gardenia perfume
licking the child-like socket of an acorn
before each is consumed.

It was not Hardy who stayed there
searching for the air-blue gown.
It was the woman who once more, secretly,
tried the dress on.

My sad descendants

O wintry ones, my sad descendants,
with snowdrops in your hands you join me
to celebrate these dark, short
days lacking a thread of sun.

Three is a virtuous number,
each time one fewer to love,
the number of fairy tales,
wishes, labours for love.

My sad descendants
who had no place in the sun,
hope brought you to mid-winter,
never to spring
or to the lazy benches of summer
and old bones.

My sad descendants
whose bones are a network of frost,
I carry your burn and your pallor,
your substance dwindled to drops.

I breathe you another pattern
since no breath warmed you from mine,
on the cold of the night window
I breathe you another pattern,

I make you outlive rosiness
and envied heartbeats.

Patrick at four years old on Bonfire Night

Cursing softly and letting the matches drop
too close to the firework box,
we light an oblation
to rough-scented autumnal gods,
shaggy as chrysanthemums;

and you, in your pearly maroon
waterproof suit, with your round
baby brows, stare upward and name
chrysanthemum fountain and silver fountain
and Catherine wheel: saints' names
like yours, Patrick, and you record them.
This morning, climbing up on my pillow,
you list saints' names guessed at from school.

They go off, one by one on the ritual plank:
jack-in-a-box, high-jump and Roman candle,
searching the currant bushes with gunpowder.

We stand in savoury fumes like pillars,
our coats dark, our slow-burning fuse lit,
and make our little bonfire with spits
for foil-wrapped potatoes and hot-dogs –

by your bedtime
the rough-scented autumnal gods
fuse with the saints and jack-lanterns.

The horse landscape

Today in a horse landscape
horses steam in the lee of thorn hedges
on soaking fields. Horses waltz
on iron poles in dank fairgrounds.

A girl in jodhpurs on Sand Bay
leads her pony over and over
jumps made of driftwood and traffic cones,

A TV blares the gabble of photofinishes.
The bookie's plastic curtain releases
punters onto the hot street
littered with King Cone papers.

In a landscape with clouds and chalk downs
and cream houses, a horse rigid as bone
glares up at kites and hang-gliders.

One eye's cut from the flowered turf:
a horse skull, whispering secrets
with wind-sighs like tapping on phone wires.

The group leader in beautiful boots
always on horse-back,
the mounted lady squinnying
down at the hunt intruders,
draw blood for their own horse landscape
and scorn horse-trading, letting the beasts mate
on scrubby fields, amongst catkins
and watery ditches.

Here's a rearing bronze horse
welded to man, letting his hands
stay free for banner and weapon –
mild shadow of Pushkin's nightmare.

Trained police horses sway on great hooves.
Riders avoid our faces, and gaze
down on our skull crowns
where the bone jigsaw cleaves.

Grooms whistle and urge
the sweaty beasts to endure battle.
We're always the poor infantry
backing off Mars field,
out of frame for the heroic riders
preserved in their horse landscape.

Thetis

Thetis, mother of all mothers
who fear the death of their children,
held down her baby Achilles
in the dark Styx

whose waters flow fast
without ripples or wave-break,
bearing little boats of paper
with matchstick masts,
returning not even a sigh
or drenched fibre to life.

Thetis, mother of all mothers
destined to outlive their children,
took Achilles by the heel
and thrust him into the Styx

so that sealed, immortal, dark-eyed,
he'd return to his white cradle
and to his willow rattle.

She might have held him less tightly
and for a while given him
wholly to the trustworthy river
which has no eddies or backwaters
and always carries its burdens onward,
she might have left him to play
on the soft grass of the river-edge.

But through the pressure-marks of her white fingers
the baby found his way forward
towards the wound he knew best.
Even while the arrow was in the wood
and the bow gleaming with leaves
the current of the Styx
faintly suckled and started
in the little flexed ankles
pressed against Thetis' damp breasts.

In the tents

Our day off, agreed by the wind
and miry fields and unburied dead,
in the tent with first light filtering
a rosy dawn which masks rain.

The rosiness rests on our damp flesh,
on armour stacked by the tent walls,
on our captain and his lolling companion.

I go down to the sea shore
to find white pebbles for games.
I look for the island, kidding myself
I see it hump through the waves.

Back in the tent it's warm, wine-smelling,
heavy with breath.
The lamp shines on the bodies
of our captain and his companion.

These are the tented days I remember
more than the battles.
This is the smell of a herbal rub
on great Achilles.
This is the blue soap-scum on the pitcher,
and cold parcels of goat-meat,
the yawning moment
late in the evening, when I step out
and see the stars alight in their same places.

Uncle Will's telegram

She kept Uncle Will's telegram
between the sheets of her wedding-album.
Her life-long imaginary future
dazzled the moment it came.

He tried the counter-top biro
and asked the post office clerk
to check the time of arrival
for ten words in block capitals.

In the levelled-down churchyard
they posed for the first photographs
while powdery grandmothers
whispered 'We wish you'
and came up with the word 'Happiness'.

She stood against laurel-black cherries
while the church dived into silence,
a great maritime creature
leaving without echoes.
At the lych-gate a tide-line
of white flowers remained.

In the Flowers the best man
read Uncle Will's telegram
and the guests lifted their glasses
shouting 'Io, Io Hymen!'

Rapunzel

Rapunzel
let down your hair,

let your strong hair
wind up the water you wish for.

All your life looking down
on bright tree-tops
your days go by quickly.

You read and you eat
in your white tower top
where sunlight fans through high
windows and far below you
bushes are matted with night.

With soft thumbprints
darkness muddles your pages.
The prince arrives,
whose noisy breathing
and sweat as he vaults your window-sill
draw you like wheat fields
on the enchanted horizontal.

He seeds your body with human fragments,
dandruff, nail-clippings, dust.
The detritus of new pleasures
falls on your waxed boards.

Your witch mother, sweeping them,
sorrowfully banishes the girl
who has let a prince clamber her.

For six years you wander the desert
from level to pale level.
At night you make a bunker to sleep in
near to the coyotes.

The ragged prince plays blind-man's-buff
to the sound of your voice singing
as you gather desert grasses
in hollows hidden from him.

Daily your wise mother
unpicks the walls of the tower.
Its stones are taken for sheep-folds,
your circle of hair
hidden beneath the brambles.

The sea skater

A skater comes to this blue pond,
his worn Canadian skates
held by the straps.

He sits on the grass
lacing stiff boots
into a wreath of effort and breath.

He tugs at the straps and they sound
as ice does when weight troubles it
and cracks bloom around stones

creaking in quiet mid-winter
mid-afternoons: a fine time for a skater.
He knows it and gauges the sun
to see how long it will be safe to skate.

Now he hisses and spins in jumps
while powder ice clings to the air
but by trade he's a long-haul skater.

Little villages, stick-like in the cold,
offer a child or a farm-worker
going his round. These watch him
go beating onward between iced alders
seawards, and so they picture him
always smoothly facing forward, foodless and waterless,
mounting the crusted waves on his skates.

In the tea house

In the tea house the usual
customers sit with their cooling
tea glasses
and new pastries
sealed at the edge
with sticky droplets.

The waitress walks off,
calves solid and shapely as vases,
leaving a juicy baba
before her favourite.

Each table has bronze or white chrysanthemums
and the copper glass-stands imperceptibly
brush each other like crickets
suddenly focussed at dusk,

but the daily newspapers
dampened by steam
don't rustle.

The tea house still has its blinds out
even though the sun is now amiably
yellow as butter

and people hurrying by raise up their faces
without abandon, briskly
talking to their companions;

no one sits out at the tables
except a travel-stained couple
thumbing a map.

The waitress reckons her cloths
watching the proprietor
while he, dark-suited, buoyant,
pauses before a customer.

Her gaze breaks upon the tea-house
like incoming water
joining sandbanks swiftly and
softly moving the pebbles,

moving the coloured sugar and coffee
to better places,
counting the pastries.

Florence in permafrost

Cold pinches the hills around Florence.
It roots out vines, truffles for lemon trees
painfully heated by charcoal
to three degrees above freezing.

A bristling fir forest
moves forward over Tuscany.
A secret wood
riddled with worm and lifeless
dust-covered branches
stings the grass and makes it flowerless,

freezing the long-closed eyelids of Romans.
They sleep entrusted to darkness
in the perpetual, placid, waveless
music of darkness.

The forest ramps over frontiers and plains
and swallows voluble Customs men
in slow ash. A wind sound
scrapes its thatching of sticks.

Blind thrushes in the wood blunder
and drop onto the brown needles.
There are no nests or singing-places.

A forest of matchwood and cheap furniture
marches in rows. Nobody harvests
its spongey woods and makes the trunks sigh
like toy soldiers giving up life.

All over Italy and northward
from fair Florence to München
and the cold city of Potsdam
the forest spreads like a pelt
on meadows, terraces, riverbanks
and the shards of brick houses.

It hides everywhere from everywhere
as each point of perspective
is gained by herds of resinous firs.

There may be human creatures
at nest in the root sockets.
They whicker words to each other
against the soughing of evergreens
while the great faces of reindeer
come grazing beside the Arno.

Missile launcher passing at night

The soft fields part in hedges, each
binds each, copse pleats
rib up the hillside.

Darkness is coming and grass
bends downward.
The cattle out all night
eat, knee-deep, invisible
unless a headlight arcs on their mild faces.

The night's damp fastens, droplet by droplet,
onto the animals.
They vibrate to the passing of a missile launcher
and stir
their patient eyelashes.

A blackbird
startled by floodlights
reproduces morning.

Cattle grids tremble and clang,
boots scrape
holly bursts against wet walls
lost at the moment of happening.

FROM

THE RAW GARDEN

(1988)

Code-breaking in the Garden of Eden

The Raw Garden is a collection of closely-related poems, which are intended to speak to, through, and even over each other. The poems draw their full effect from their setting; they feed from each other, even when the link is as mild as an echo of phrasing or cadence.

It is now possible to insert new genes into a chromosomal pattern. It is possible to feed in new genetic material, or to remove what is seen as faulty or damaged material. The basic genetic code is contained in DNA (deoxyribonucleic acid), and its molecular structure is the famous double helix, so called because it consists of two complementary spirals which match each other like the halves of a zip. Naturally-occurring enzymes can be used to split the double strand, and to insert new material. The separate strands are then recombined to form the complete DNA helix. By this process of gene-splicing a new piece of genetic information can be inserted into a living organism, and can be transmitted to the descendants of the organism.

It seems to me that there is an echo of this new and revolutionary scientific process in the way each poet feeds from the material drawn together in a long poetic tradition, "breaks" it with his or her individual creative voice, and re-combines it through new poems.

One thing I have tried to do in these poems is to explore the effect which these new possibilities of genetic manipulation may have on our concept of what is natural and what is unnatural. If we can not follow Romantic poets in their assumption of a massive, unmalleable landscape which moulds the human creatures living upon it and provides them with a constant, stable frame of reference, then how do we look at landscape and at the "natural"? We are used to living in a profoundly human-made landscape. As I grew up I realised that even such apparently wild places as moors and commons were the product of human decisions and work: people had cut down trees, grazed animals, acquired legal rights. But still this knowledge did not interfere with my sense that these places were natural.

The question might be, what does it take to disturb the sense of naturalness held by the human being in his or her, landscape? Is there a threshold beyond which a person revolts at a feeling that changedness has gone too far? Many of these poems focus on highly manipulated landscapes and outcrops of "nature", and on the harmonies and revulsions formed between them and the people living among them.

Perhaps the Garden of Eden embodies some yearning to print down an idea of the static and the predictable over our knowledge that we have to accept perpetual changeability. The code of the Garden of Eden has been broken open an infinite number of times. Now we are faced with a still greater potential for change, since we have acquired knowledge of the double helix structure of DNA. If the Garden of Eden really exists it does so moment by moment, fragmented and tough, cropping up like a fan of buddleia high up in the gutter of a deserted warehouse, or in a heap of frozen cabbages becoming luminous in the reflected light off roadside snow. This Garden of Eden propagates itself in strange ways, some of which find parallels in far-fetched horticultural techniques such as air layering, or growing potatoes in a mulch of rotted seaweed on white sand. I hope that these poems do not seem to hanker back to a prelapsarian state of grace. If I want to celebrate anything, it is resilience, adaptability, and the power of improvisation.

Seal run

The potatoes come out of the earth bright
as if waxed, shucking their compost,

and bob against the palm of my hand
like the blunt muzzles of seals swimming.

Slippy and pale in the washing-up bowl
they bask, playful, grown plump
in banks of seaweed on white sand,

seaweed hauled from brown circles
set in transparent waters off Easdale

all through the sun-fanned West Highland midnights
when the little potatoes are seeding there
to make necklaces under the mulch,
torques and amulets in their burial place.

The seals quiver, backstroking
for pure joy of it, down to the tidal
slim mouth of the loch,

they draw their lips back, their blunt whiskers
tingle at the inspout of salt water

then broaching the current they roll
off between islands and circles of oarweed.

At noon the sea-farmer
turns back his blanket of weed
and picks up potatoes like eggs
from their fly-swarming nest,

too fine for the sacks, so he puts them in boxes
and once there they smell earthy.

At noon the seals nose up the rocks
to pile there, sun-dazed,
back against belly, island on island.

and sleep, shivering like dogs
against the tug of the stream
flowing on south past Campbelltown.

The man's hands rummage about still
to find what is full-grown there.
Masts on the opposite shore ring faintly

disturbing themselves, and make him look up.
Hands down and still moving
he works on, his fingers at play blinded,
his gaze roving the ripe sea-loch.

Wild strawberries

What I get I bring home to you:
a dark handful, sweet-edged,
dissolving in one mouthful.

I bother to bring them for you
though they're so quickly over,
pulpless, sliding to juice,

a grainy rub on the tongue
and the taste's gone. If you remember
we were in the woods at wild strawberry time

and I was making a basket of dockleaves
to hold what you'd picked,
but the cold leaves unplaited themselves

and slid apart, and again unplaited themselves
until I gave up and ate wild strawberries
out of your hands for sweetness.

I lipped at your palm –
the little salt edge there,
the tang of money you'd handled.

As we stayed in the wood, hidden,
we heard the sound system below us
calling the winners at Chepstow,
faint as the breeze turned.

The sun came out on us, the shade blotches
went hazel: we heard names
bubble like stock-doves over the woods

as jockeys in stained silks gentled
those sweat-dark, shuddering horses
down to the walk.

A mortgage on a pear tree

A pear tree stands in its own maze.
It does not close its blossom all night
but holds out branchfuls of cool
wide-open flowers. Its slim leaves look black
and stir like tongues in the lamp-light.

It was here before the houses were built.
The owner grew wasteland and waited for values to rise.
The builders swerved a boundary sideways
to cup the tree in a garden. When they piled rubble
it was a soft cairn mounting the bole.

The first owner of the raw garden
came out and walked on the clay clods.
There was the pear tree, bent down
with small blunt fruits, each wide where the flower was,
shaped like a medlar, but sweet.

The ground was dense with fermenting pears,
half trodden to pulp, half eaten.
She could not walk without slipping.

Slowly she walked in her own maze,
sleepy, feeling the blood seep
down her cold fingers, down the spread branch
of veins which trails to the heart,

and remembered how she'd stood under a tree
holding out arms, with two school-friends.
It was the fainting-game,
played in the dinner-hour from pure boredom,
never recalled since. For years this was growing
to meet her, and now she's signed for her own
long mortgage over the pear tree
and is the gainer of its accrued beauty,

but when she goes into her bedroom
and draws her curtains against a spring night
the pear tree does not close its white blossom.
The flowers stay open with slim leaves flickering around them:
touched and used, they bear fruit.

A pæony truss on Sussex Place

Restless, the pæony truss tosses about
in a destructive spring wind.
Already its inner petals are white
without one moment of sun-warmed expansion.

The whole bunch of the thing looks poor
as a stout bare-legged woman in November
slopping her mules over the post office step
to cash a slip of her order book.

The wind rips round the announced site
for inner city conversion: this is the last tough
bit of the garden, with one lilac
half sheared-off and half blooming.

The AIDS ad is defaced and the Australian
lager-bright billboard smirks down
on wind-shrivelled passersby who stayed put
to vote in the third Thatcher election.

The porch of the Elim Pentecostal Church brightens
as a woman in crimson and white suit
steps out, pins her hat down
then grasps the hands of her wind-tugged grandchildren.

Permafrost

For all frozen things –
my middle finger that whitens
from its old, ten-minute frostbite,

for black, slimy potatoes
left in the clamp,
for darkness and cold like cloths
over the cage,

for permafrost, lichen crusts
nuzzled by reindeer,
the tender balance of decades
null as a vault.

For all frozen things –
the princess and princes
staring out of their bunker
at the original wind,

for NATO survivors in nuclear moonsuits
whirled from continent to continent

like Okies in bumpy Fords
fleeing the dustbowl.

For all frozen things –
snowdrops and Christmas roses
blasted down to the germ
of their genetic zip-code.

They fly by memory –
cargo of endless winter,
clods of celeriac, chipped
turnips, lanterns at ten a.m.

in the gloom of a Finnish market lace;
flowers under glass, herring,
little wizened apples.

For all frozen things –
the nipped fish in a mess of ice,
the uncovered galleon
tossed from four centuries of memory,

or nuclear snowsuits bouncing on dust,
trapped on the rough ride of the earth's surface,
on the rough swing of its axis,

like moon-men lost on the moon
watching the earth's green flush

tremble and perish.

At Cabourg

Later my stepson will uncover a five-inch live shell
from a silted pool on the beach at St Côme. It is complete
with brass cap and a date on it: nineteen forty-three.
We'll look it up in the dictionary, take it
to show at the Musée de la Libération
– ce petit obus – but once they unwrap it
they'll drop the polite questions and scramble
full tilt for the Gendarmerie opposite.
The gendarmes will peer through its cradle of polythene
gingerly, laughing. One's at the phone
already – he gestures – 'Imagine! Let's tell them
we've got a live shell here in the Poste!'

Of course this will have happened before.
They'll have it exploded, there'll be no souvenir shell-case,
and we'll be left with our photographs
taken with a camera which turns out to be broken.

Later we'll be at the Château Fontaine-Henry
watching sleek daughters in jodhpurs come in from the fields.
I'll lie back in my green corduroy coat, and leave,
faint, to drive off through fields of sunflowers
without visiting the rooms we've paid for.
Madame will have her fausse-couche,
her intravenous injections, her glass ampoules,
in a room which is all bed
and smells of medicinal alcohol and fruit.
The children will play on the beach, a little forlornly,
in the wind which gusts up out of nowhere.

Later we'll see our friends on their lightweight bicycles
freewheeling tiredly downhill to Asnelles.
Their little son, propped up behind them
will glide past, silent, though he alone sees us.

But now we are on the beach at Cabourg,
stopped on our walk to look where the sky's whitening
over the sea beyond Dives. Now a child squawks
and races back as a wave slaps over his shorts' hem

to where a tanned woman with naked breasts
fidgets her baby's feet in the foam
straight down from the Boulevard Marcel Proust.

Ploughing the roughlands

It's not the four-wheeled drive crawler
spitting up dew and herbs,

not Dalapon followed by dressings
of dense phosphates,

nor ryegrass greening behind wire as behind glass,

not labourers wading in moonsuits
through mud gelded by paraquat –

but now, the sun-yellow, sky-blue
vehicles mount the pale chalk,

the sky bowls on the white hoops
and white breast of the roughland,

the farmer with Dutch eyes
guides forward the quick plough.

Now, flush after flush of Italian ryegrass
furs up the roughland

with its attentive, bright,
levelled-off growth –

pale monoculture
sweating off rivers of filth

fenced by the primary
colours of crawler and silo.

The land pensions

The land pensions, like rockets
shoot off from wheat with a soft yellow
flame-bulb: a rook or a man in black
flaps upwards with white messages.

On international mountains and spot markets
little commas of wheat translate.
The stony ground's pumped to a dense fire
by the flame-throwing of chemicals.
On stony ground the wheat can ignite
its long furls.

The soft rocket of land pensions flies
and is seen in Japan, covering
conical hills with its tender stars:
now it is firework time, remembrance
and melt-down of autumn chrysanthemums.

On bruised fields above Brighton
grey mould laces the wheat harvest.
The little rockets are black. Land pensions
fasten on silos elsewhere, far off.

Market men flicker and skulk like eels
half-way across earth to breed.
On thin chipped flint-and-bone land
a nitrate river laces the grey wheat
pensioning off chalk acres.

A dream of wool

Decoding a night's dreams
of sheepless uplands
the wool-merchant clings to the wool churches,

to trade with the Low Countries,
to profitable, downcast
ladies swathed in wool sleeves

whose plump, light-suffused faces
gaze from the triptychs he worships.

Sheep ticks, maggoty tails and foot-rot
enter his tally of dense beasts, walking
with a winter's weight on their backs

through stubborn pasture
they graze to a hairsbreadth.

From the turf of the Fire Hills
the wool-merchant trawls
sheep for the marsh markets.
They fill mist with their thin cries –

circular eddies, bemusing
the buyers of mutton
from sheep too wretched to fleece.

In the right angle of morning sunshine
the aerial photographer
shoots from the blue,

decodes a landscape
of sheepless uplands
and ploughed drove roads,

decodes the airstream, the lapis lazuli
coat for many compacted skeletons
seaming the chalk by the sea.

New crops

O engines
flying over the light, barren
as shuttles, thrown over a huge
woof

crossply
of hedgeless snail tracks,
you are so high,

you've felled the damp crevices

you've felled the boulder-strewn meadow
the lichen
the strong plum tree.

O engines
swaying your rubber batons
on pods, on ripe lupins,
on a chameleon terrace
of greenlessness,

you're withdrawn from a sea
of harvests, you're the foreshore

of soaked soil leaching
undrinkable streams.

Shadows of my mother against a wall

The wood-pigeon rolls soft notes off its breast
in a tree which grows by a fence.
The smell of creosote,
easy as wild gum
oozing from tree boles
keeps me awake. A thunderstorm
heckles the air.

I step into a bedroom
pungent with child's sleep,
and lift the potty and pile of picture books
so my large shadow
crosses his eyes.

Sometimes at night, expectant,
I think I see the shadow of my mother
bridge a small house of enormous rooms.
Here are white, palpable walls
and stories of my grandmother:
the old hours of tenderness I missed.

Air layering

The rain was falling down in slow pulses
between the horse-chestnuts, as if it would set root there.

It was a slate-grey May evening
luminous with new leaves.
I was at a talk on the appearances of Our Lady
these past five years at Medjugorje.
We sat in a small room in the Presbytery:
the flow of the video scratched, the raindrop
brimmed its meniscus upon the window
from slant runnel to sill.

Later I watched a programme on air layering.
The round rootball steadied itself
high as a chaffinch nest, and then deftly
the gardener severed the new plant.
She knew its wounded stem would have made roots there.

The argument

It was too hot, that was the argument.
I had to walk a mile with my feet flaming
from brown sandals and sun.

Now the draggling shade of the privet made me to dawdle,
now soft tarmac had to be crossed.
I was lugging an old school-bag –

it was so hot the world was agape with it.
One limp rose fell as I passed.

An old witch sat in her front garden
under the spokes of a black umbrella
lashed to her kitchen chair.
God was in my feet as I fled past her.

Everyone I knew was so far away.
The yellow glob of my ice cream melted and spread.
I bought it with huge pennies, held up.
'A big one this time!' the man said,
so I ate on though it cloyed me.
It was for fetching the bread
one endless morning before Bank Holiday.

I was too young, that was the argument,
and had to propitiate everyone:
the man with the stroke, and the burnt lady
whose bared, magical teeth made me
smile if I could –
Oh the cowardice of my childhood!

The peach house

The dry glasshouse is almost empty.
A few pungent geraniums with lost markings
lean in their pots.

It is nothing but a cropping place for sun
on cold Northumbrian July days.

The little girl, fresh from suburbia,
cannot believe in the peaches she finds here.
They are green and furry as monkeys –
she picks them and drops them.

All the same they are matched to the word peach
and must mean more than she sees. She will post them
unripe in a tiny envelope
to her eight-year-old class-mates, and write
carefully in the ruled-up spaces:
'Where we are the place is a palace.'

A meditation on the glasshouses

The bald glasshouses stretch here for miles.
For miles air-vents open like wings.

This is the land of reflections, of heat
flagging from.mirror to mirror. Here cloches
force on the fruit by weeks, while pulses
of light run down the chain of glasshouses
and blind the visitors this Good Friday.

The daffodil pickers are spring-white.
Their neat heads in a fuzz of sun
stoop to the buds, make leafless
bunches of ten for Easter.

A white thumb touches the peat
but makes no print. This is the soil-less
Eden of glasshouses, heat-stunned.

he haunting of Epworth

Epworth Rectory was the childhood home of John Wesley.
In December 1716 the house was possessed by a poltergeist;
after many unsuccessful attempts at exorcism the spirit,
nicknamed 'Old Jeffery' by the little Wesley girls, left
of its own accord.

Old Jeffery begins his night music.
The girls, sheathed in their brick skin,
giggle with terror. The boys are all gone
out to the world, 'continually sinning',
their graces exotic and paid for.

Old Jeffery rummages pitchforks
up the back chimney. The girls
open the doors to troops of exorcists
who plod back over the Isle of Axeholme
balked by the house. The scrimmage
of iron, shattering windows, and brickwork
chipped away daily is birdsong
morning and evening, or sunlight
into their unsunned lives.

Old Jeffery tires of the house slowly.
He knocks the back of the connubial bed
where nineteen Wesleys, engendered in artlessness
swarm, little ghosts of themselves.
The girls learn to whistle his music.

The house bangs like a side-drum
as Old Jeffery goes out of it. Daughters
in white wrappers mount to the windows, sons
coming from school make notes – the wildness
goes out towards Epworth and leaves nothing
but the bald house straining on tiptoe
after its ghost.

Preaching at Gwennap

*Gwennap Pit is a natural amphitheatre
in Cornwall, where John Wesley preached.*

Preaching at Gwennap, silk
ribbons unrolling far off,
the unteachable turquoise and green
coast dropping far off,

preaching at Gwennap, where thermals revolve
to the bare lip, where granite
breaks its uneasy backbone,
where a great natural theatre, cut
to a hairsbreadth, sends back each cadence,

preaching at Gwennap to a child asleep
while the wide plain murmurs, and prayers
ply on the void, tendered like cords
over the pit's brim.
               Off to one side
a horse itches and dreams. Its saddle
comes open, stitch after stitch,

while the tired horse, standing for hours
flicks flies from its arse
and eats through the transfiguration –
old sobersides
mildly eschewing more light.

On circuit from Heptonstall Chapel

*'Tis not everyone could bear these things, but I bless God,
my wife is less concerned with suffering them than
I in writing them.'*

SAMUEL WESLEY, father of John Wesley,
writing of his wife Susanna

The mare with her short legs heavily mud-caked
plods, her head down
over the unearthly grasses,
the burning salt-marshes,

through sharp-sided marram and mace
with the rim of the tide's eyelid
out to the right.

The reed-cutters go home
whistling sharply, crab-wise
beneath their dense burdens,

the man on the mare weighs heavy, his broadcloth
shiny and worn, his boots dangling
six inches from ground.
He clenches his buttocks to ease them,
shifts Bible and meat,

thinks of the congregation
gathered beyond town,
wind-whipped, looking for warm
words from his dazed lips.

No brand from the burning;
a thick man with a day's travel
caked on him like salt,

a preacher, one of those scattered like thistle
from the many-angled home chapel
facing all ways on its slabbed upland.

US 1st Division Airborne Ranger at rest in Honduras

The long arm hangs flat to his lap.
The relaxed wrist-joint is tender, shade-
cupped at the base of the thumb.

That long, drab line of American cloth,
those flat brows knitting a crux,
the close-shaven scalp, cheeks, jawbone and lips

rest in abeyance here, solid impermanence
like the stopped breath of a runner swathed up
in tinfoil bodybag, back from the front.

He rests, coloured like August foliage and earth
when the wheat's cropped, and the massive harvesters
go out on hire elsewhere,

his single-lens perspex eyeswield pushed up, denting
the folds of his skull stubble, his cap
shading his eyes which are already shaded
by bone. His pupils are shuttered,
the lenses widening inwards,
notions of a paling behind them.

One more for the beautiful table

Dense slabs of braided-up lupins –
someone's embroidery – Nan,
liking the blue,

one more for the beautiful table
with roses and handkerchiefs, seams
on the web of fifty five-year-olds' life-spans.

New, tough little stitches
run on the torn
wedding head-dresses.
No one can count them
back to the far-off
ghosts of the children's conceptions.

Those party days:

one more for the beautiful table

the extinction of breath in a sash.

What looks and surprises!
Nan on her bad legs
resumes the filminess of petals
and quotes blood pricks and blood stains

faded to mauve and to white and to crisp
brown drifts beneath bare sepals –

look, they have washed out.

Lambkin

(a poem in mother dialect)

That's better, he says, he says
that's better.

Dense slabs of braided-up lupins –
someone's embroidery – Nan,
liking the blue,

Oh you're a tinker, that's what you are,
a little tinker, a tinker, that's what you are.

One more for the beautiful table
with roses and handkerchiefs, seams
on the web of fifty five-year-olds' life-spans.

Come on now, come on, come on now,
come on, come on, come on now,

new tough little stitches
run on the torn
wedding head-dresses.
The children count them
back to the far-off
ghosts of their own conceptions.

Oh you like that, I know, yes,
you kick those legs, you kick them,
you kick those fat legs then.

Those party days

one more for the beautiful table

set out in the hall.

You mustn't have any tears, you're my good boy
aren't you my little good boy.

What looks and surprises!
Nan on her bad legs
resumes the filminess of petals,

she'll leave it to Carlie
her bad spice.

Let's wipe those tears, let's wipe off all those tears.
That's better, he says, he says
that's right.

She quotes blood pricks and bloodstains
faded to mauve and to white and to crisp
brown drifts beneath bare sepals –

look, they have washed out.

The green recording light falters
as if picking up voices

it's pure noise grain and nothing more human.
It's all right lambkin I've got you I've got you.

Dublin 1971

The grass looks different in another country.
By a shade more or a shade less, it startles
as love does in the sharply-tinged landscape
of sixteen to eighteen. When it is burnt
midsummer and lovers have learned to make love
with scarcely a word said, then they see nothing
but what is closest: an eyelash tonight,
the slow spread of a sweat stain,
the shoe-sole of the other as he walks off
watched from the mattress.

The top deck of the bus babbles with diplomats'
children returning from school, their language
an overcast August sky which can't clear.
Each syllable melting to static
troubles the ears of strangers, no stranger
but less sure than the stick-limbed children.
With one silvery, tarnishing ring between them
they walk barefoot past the Martello tower
at Sandymount, and wish the sea clearer,
the sun for once dazzling, fledged
from its wet summer nest of cloud-strips.

They make cakes of apple peel and arrowroot
and hear the shrieks of bold, bad seven-year-old Seamus
who holds the pavement till gone midnight
for all his mother's forlorn calling.
The freedom of no one related for thousands of miles,
the ferry forever going backward and forward
from rain runnel to drain cover...

The grass looks different in another country,
sudden and fresh, waving, unfurling
the last morning they see it, as they go down
to grey Dún Laoghaire by taxi.
They watch the slate rain coming in eastward
pleating the sea not swum in,
blotting the Ballsbridge house with its soft sheets
put out in the air to sweeten.

The hard-hearted husband

'Has she gone then?' they asked,
stepping round the back of the house
whose cat skulked in the grass.

She'd left pegs dropped in the bean-row,
and a mauve terrycloth babygrow
stirred on the line as I passed.

Her damsons were ripe and her sage was in flower,
her roses tilted from last night's downpour,
her sweetpeas and sunflowers leaned anywhere.

'She got sick of it, then,' they guessed,
and wondered if the torn-up paper
might be worth reading, might be a letter.

'It was the bills got her,' they knew,
seeing brown envelopes sheared with the white
in a jar on the curtainless windowsill,

some of them sealed still, as if she was through
with trying to pay, and would sit, chilled,
ruffling and arranging them like flowers
in the long dusks while the kids slept upstairs.

The plaster was thick with her shadows,
damp and ready to show
how she lived there and lay fallow

and how she stood at her window
and watched tall pylons stride down the slope
sizzling faintly, stepping away
as she now suddenly goes,

too stubborn to be ghosted at thirty.
She will not haunt here. She picks up her dirty
warm children and takes them

down to the gate which she lifts as it whines
and sets going a thin cry in her.
He was hard-hearted and no good to her
they say now, grasping the chance to be kind.

Malta

The sea's a featureless blaze.
On photographs nothing comes out
but glare, with that scarlet-rimmed fishing boat
far-off, lost to the lens.

At noon a stiff-legged tourist in shorts
steps, camera poised. He's stilted
as a flamingo, pink-limbed.

Icons of Malta gather around him.
He sweats as a procession passes
and women with church-dark faces
brush him as if he were air.

He holds a white crocheted dress
to give to his twelve-year-old daughter
who moons in the apartment, sun-sore.
The sky's tight as a drum, hard
to breathe in, hard to walk under.

He would not buy 'bikini for daughter'
though the man pressed him, with plump fingers
spreading out scraps of blue cotton.

Let her stay young, let her know nothing.
Let her body remain skimpy and sudden.
His wife builds arches of silence over her
new breasts and packets of tampons marked 'slender'.
At nights, when they think she's asleep,
they ache in the same places
but never louder than a whisper.

He watches more women melt into a porch.
Their white, still laundry flags from window to window
while they are absent, their balconies blank.

At six o'clock, when he comes home and snicks
his key in the lock so softly neither will catch it
he hears one of them laugh.
They are secret in the kitchen, talking of nothing,
strangers whom anyone might love.

Candlemas

Snowdrops, Mary's tapers,
barely alight in the grey shadows,

Candlemas in a wet February,
the soil clodded and frostless,
the quick blue shadows of snowlight again missed.

The church candles' mass
yellow as mothering bee cells,
melts to soft puddles of wax,

the snowdrops, with crisp ruffs
and green spikes clearing the leaf debris

are an unseen nebula
caught by a swinging telescope,

white tapers
blooming in structureless dusk.

Pilgrims

Let us think that we are pilgrims
in furs on this bleak water.
The *Titanic*'s lamps hang on its sides like fruit
on lit cliffs. We're shriven for rescue.

The sea snaps at our caulking.
We bend to our oars and praise God
and flex our fingers to bring
a drowned child out from the tarpaulin.

We're neither mothers nor fathers, but children,
fearful and full of trust,
lamblike as the *Titanic* goes down
entombing its witnesses.

We row on in a state of grace
in our half-empty lifeboats, sailing
westward for America, pilgrims,
numb to the summer-like choir
of fifteen hundred companions.

An Irish miner in Staffordshire

On smooth buttercup fields
the potholers sink down like dreams
close to Roman lead-mining country.

I sink the leafless shaft of an hydrangea twig
down through the slippy spaces I've made for it.
Dusted with hormone powder, moist,
its fibrous stem splays into root.

I graze the soft touches of compost
and wash them off easily, balled
under the thumb – clean dirt.
There's the man who gave me my Irish name

still going down, wifeless, that miner
who shafted the narrow cuffs of the earth
as if it was this he came for.

FROM

SHORT DAYS, LONG NIGHTS

(1991)

Those shady girls

Those shady girls on the green side of the street,
those far-from-green girls who keep to the shade,
those shady girls in mysterious suits
with their labels half-showing
as the cream flap of the jacket swings open,
those girls kicking aside the front-panelled pleats
of their cream suits with cerise lapels,

those on-coming girls,
those girls swinging pearly umbrellas
as tightly-sheathed as tulips in bud
from an unscrupulous street-seller,
those girls in cream and cerise suits
which mark if you touch them,
those girls with their one-name appointments
who walk out of the sunshine.

The dream-life of priests

Do they wake careless and warm
with light on the unwashed windows
and a perpetual smell of bacon,

do their hearts sink at today's martyr
with his unpronounceable name
and strange manner of execution?

Do they wake out of the darkness
with hearts thudding like ours
and reach for the souvenir lamp-switch

then shove a chair against the door
and key facts into the desk-top computer
while cold rattles along the corridor?

Do they cry out in sleep
at some barely-crushed thought,
some failure to see the joke,

or do they rest in their dreams
along the surface of the water
like a bevy of dragonflies

slack and blue in the shallows
whirring among reed-mace and water-forget-me-not
while the ripples cluck?

Do they wake in ordinary time
to green curtains slapping the frame
of a day that'll cloud later on,

to cars nudging and growling for space,
to a baptismal mother, wan with her eagerness
and her sleepless, milk-sodden nights?

Do they reach and stroke the uneven plaster
and sniff the lime-blossom threading
like silk through the room,

or do they wait, stretched out like babies
in the gold of its being too early
with sun on their ceilings wobbling like jelly

while their housekeepers jingle the milk-bottles
and cry 'Father!' in sixty-year-old voices
and scorch toast with devotion –

do they sense the milk in the pan rising
then dive with their blue chins, blundering
through prayer under their honeycomb blankets?

Sisters leaving before the dance

Sisters leaving before the dance,
before the caller gets drunk
or the yellow streamers unreel
looping like ribbons
here and there on the hair of the dancers,

sisters at the turn of the stairs
as the sound system
one-twos, as the squeezebox
mewed in its case

is slapped into breath, and that scrape
of the tables shoved back for the dance
burns like the strike of a match
in the cup of two hands.
Ripe melons and meat

mix in the binbags with cake
puddled in cherry-slime, wind
heavy with tar
blows back the yard door, and I'm

caught with three drinks in my hands
on the stairs looking up
at the sisters leaving before the dance,
not wishing to push past them
in their white broderie anglaise and hemmed

skirts civilly drawn
to their sides to make room
for the big men in suits,
and the girls in cerise

dance-slippers and cross-backed dresses
who lead the way up
and take charge of the tickets, and yet
from their lips cantaloupe
fans as they speak

in bright quick murmurs between
a violin ghosting a tune
and the kids in the bar downstairs
begging for Coke, peaky but certain.

The sisters say their *good nights*
and all the while people stay bunched
on the stairs going up, showing respect
for the small words of the ones leaving,
the ones who don't stay for the dancing.

One sister twists a white candle
waxed in a nest of hydrangeas –
brick-red and uncommon, flowers
she really can't want – she bruises the limp

warm petals with crisp fingers
and then poises her sandal
over the next non-slip stair
so the dance streams at her heels
in the light of a half-shut door.

On not writing certain poems

You put your hand over mine and whispered
'There he is, laying against the pebbles' –
you wouldn't point for the shadow
stirring the trout off his bed
where he sculled the down-running water,

and the fish lay there, unbruised
by the soft knuckling of the river-bed
or your stare which had found him out.

Last night I seemed to be walking
with something in my hand, earthward, down-
dropping as lead, unburnished –

a plate perhaps or a salver
with nothing on it or offered
but its own shineless composure.

I have it here on my palm, the weight
settled, spreading through bone
until my wrist tips backward, pulled down

as if my arm was laid in a current
of eel-dark water – that thrum
binding the fingers – arrow-like –

Privacy of rain

Rain. A plump splash
on tense, bare skin.
Rain. All the May leaves
run upward, shaking.

Rain. A first touch
at the nape of the neck.
Sharp drops kick the dust, white
downpours shudder
like curtains, rinsing
tight hairdos to innocence.

I love the privacy of rain,
the way it makes things happen
on verandahs, under canopies
or in the shelter of trees
as a door slams and a girl runs out
into the black-wet leaves.
By the brick wall an iris
sucks up the rain
like intricate food, its tongue
sherbetty, furred.

Rain. All the May leaves
run upward, shaking.
On the street bud-silt
covers the windscreens.

Dancing man

That lake lies along the shore
like a finger down my cheek,

its waters lull and collapse
dark as pomegranates,

the baby crawls on the straw
in the shadow-map of his father's chair

while the priest talks things over
and light dodges across his hair.

There's a lamp lit in the shed
and a fire on, and a man drinking

spiritus fortis he's made for himself.
But on the floor of the barn

the dancing man is beginning to dance.
First a beat from the arch of his foot

as he stands upright, a neat
understatement of all that's in him

and he lowers his eyes to her
as if it's nothing, nothing –

but she has always wanted him.
Her baby crawls out from the chairs

and rolls in his striped vest laughing
under the feet of the dancers

so she must dance over him
toe to his cheek, heel to his hair,

as she melts to the man dancing.
They are talking and talking over there –

the priest sits with his back to her
for there's no malice in him

and her husband glistens like the sun
through the cypress-flame of the man dancing

In the shed a blackbird
has left three eggs which might be kumquats –

they are so warm. One of them's stirring –
who said she had deserted them?

In the orchard by the barn
there are three girls wading,

glossy, laughing at something,
they spin a bucket between them,

glowing, they are forgotten –
something else is about to happen.

At Cabourg II

The bathers, where are they? The sea is quite empty,
lapsed from its task of rinsing the white beach.

The promenade has a skein of walkers, four to the mile,
like beads threaded on the long Boulevard in front of the flowers.

Shutters are all back on the bankers' fantasy houses,
but the air inside is glassy as swimming-pool water,

no one breathes there or silts it with movement,
Out of the kitchen a take-away steam rises:

the bankers are having sushi in honour of their guests
who are here, briefly, to buy 'an impressionist picture'.

A boy is buried up to his neck in sand
but the youth leader stops another who pretends to piss on him.

The rest draw round, they have got something helpless:
his head laid back on its platter of curls.

With six digging, he's out in a minute.
They oil his body with Ambre Solaire,

two boys lay him across their laps, a third
wipes at his feet then smiles up enchantingly.

Baron Hardup

I see the boys at the breakwater
straighten now, signalling friends,
and the little imperious one who is just not
dinted at the back of the arms
with child-like softness
sticks up his thumb to mark the next leap.

This far off it's peaceful to watch them
while I'm walking ahead barefoot
on a wide, grey Norman promenade,
thinking of the Baron de Charlus
not in his wheelchair but younger,
bumbling into seduction in a hot courtyard,

tipped upside-down like a sand-timer,
labelled implacably – 'the invert'
caught at the wide-striped
dawn years of the century
where the candy of skirts blows inward and outward
to a pure, bellying offshore wind.

The beautiful line of his coat ripples –
he's Baron Hardup with dreams tupping
like pantomime horses – he fixes his eyeglass
and glares at the waves with passionate indecisiveness
as if to stop, or not stop, their irregular fall,
while the boys figure what he is good for.

Nearly May Day

After a night jagged by guard-dogs and nightingales
I sit to be videoed
at the corner of this carved balcony
where ten o'clock sun falls
past the curve of the Berlin Wall.
It's nearly May Day.
Just here there's a double wall –
a skin of concrete, a skin of stone
the colour of the Alsatians.

My feet shift on the slats.
I want to comb my hair straight.
I have my back
to a wood in the closed zone –
an orchard's bright pelt
sparkling with blossom tips.
Bees fly in purposeful zigzags
over the Wall, tracing their map
of air and nectar.
Each day they fly through the spoors
of air-wiping floodlights now
sheathed in the watch-towers
to this one apple tree
which makes a garden of itself
under the balcony.

I have my back to the church.
Its roof glows in the gaps
where slate after slate's peeled off.
I have my back to the porch
with its red lining of valerian,
its sound like a cough
as the doors squeeze themselves shut.
Katja unrolls cable
over the balcony rail.
A double wiring of roses
straddles the pews
in a hamlet which is the other half of here,
clear and suggestive as a mirror.

They say nobody lives there
but guards' wives and children.
You rarely see them,
they melt into the woods like foxes
but you hear their motorbikes miles off
clutching the road surface.
You might hear the guards' wives say
'Let the kids have the grapes'
just as the nightingales insist
for hours when you can't sleep.

This hamlet's like something I've dreamed
in a dream broken by rain,
with its lilac and dull green
tenderly shifting leaves,
its woodpiles,
its watched inhabitants,
wives of the guards
who have between them a little son
in a too-tight yellow jersey
flashing along their own balcony.

He runs from his steep-roofed home
to scrabble onto his tricycle
and race with fat frantic legs pedalling
the few square metres marked by the wives
with a shield-square of clothes-line
where they're forever hanging things out
while my back's turned.
I study the guards' underpants
and wish I still smoked
so I could blow smoke-rings
from the balcony of Jagdschloss Glienicke
past the flowering jaws of the apple tree
over complicated roof-shells
to the child himself.
I'd wave, holding the cigarette
cupped behind my back.

Any time they choose
people are changing Deutschmarks
for a tick on cheap paper,
a day-trip to the East
to buy Bulgarian church music
and butter at half-price,
to check their faces in a mirror
and get it all on video.
to walk through a map of mirrors
into the other half of here.

There's mist on the Glienicke bridge.
The flags are limp.
There's nothing flying at all –
not a flag, not an aeroplane
racing down safe corridors.

It's nearly May Day.
A riot's ripening in Kreuzberg.
If this is Spring, it's going on elsewhere
grasping horse-chestnut buds
in sticky hands
warm and forgetful
as a child who buries himself
for joy in Pankow's warm sands.

[September 1989]

Three workmen with blue pails

Three workmen with blue pails
swerve past an election poster
wrapped round a lamp-post pillar,

signed with a single carnation
and a name for each ward.
The workmen guffaw –

it's five past three on a small street
which traipses off Unter den Linden
deep into East Berlin.

Short, compact and bored
they tramp over the slats
where the pavement's torn up.

One of them's telling a joke.
They swing on under a banner
for a play by Harold Pinter –

stretched linen, four metres wide
and at least two workmen tall,
spread on a ten-metre wall –

the play's *The Dumb Waiter*.
They go on past a kindergarten
which is tipping out children,

past banks with bullet-holes in them,
past an industrial shoal
of tower-block homes

to the second-right turn
where the pulse of street-life picks up,
where there are people and shops.

Ahead, a queue forms
as a café rattles itself open
and starts to serve out ice cream.

Inside his treacle-brown frame
a young man flickers and smiles
as he fans out the biscuit-shells –

already half the ice cream's gone
and the waiter teases the children
with cold smoke from a new can.

Seeds stick to their tongues –
gooseberry, cloudberry – chill,
grainy and natural.

Shoving their caps back
the workmen join on
and move forward in line

for what's over. Tapping light coins
they move at a diagonal
to a blue, skew-whiff ditched Trabbi.

Brown coal

The room creaked like a pair of lungs
and the fire wouldn't go
till we held up the front page for it.
All the while the news was on

that day they wired up the Wall
while I was swimming on newspaper –
a cold rustle of words
to the wheezing of my sister.

I caught the fringe of her scarf
in winter smogs after school
as she towed me through the stutter
of high-lamped Ford Populars

and down the mouth of the railway tunnel
into water-pocked walls
and the dense sulphurous hollows
of nowhere in particular.

It was empty but for smog.
Coughing through our handkerchiefs
we walked eerily, lammed
at the brickwork, picked ourselves up.

I walked through nowhere last April
into a mist of brown coal,
sulphur emissions, diesel
stopped dead at the Wall,

the whiff of dun Trabants
puttering north/south
past a maze of roadworks,
leaving hours for us to cross

in the slow luxury of strolling
as the streets knit themselves up
to become a city again.
By instinct I kept my mouth shut

and breathed like one of us girls
in our "identical-twin" coats,
listening out for rare cars,
coal at the back of our throats –

it was England in the fifties,
half-blind with keeping us warm,
so I was completely at ease
in a small street off Unter Den Linden

as a fire-door behind wheezed
and Berlin creaked like two lungs.

Safe period

Your dry voice from the centre of the bed
asks 'Is it safe?'

and I answer for the days as if I owned them.
Practised at counting, I rock
the two halves of the month like a cradle.

The days slip over their stile
and expect nothing. They are just days,

and we're at it again, thwarting
souls from the bodies they crave.

They'd love to get into this room
under the yellow counterpane
we've torn to make a child's cuddly,

they'd love to slide into the sheets
between soft, much-washed
flannelette fleece,

they'd love to be here in the moulded spaces
between us, where there is no room,

but we don't let them. They fly about gustily,
noisy as our own children.

Big barbershop man

Big barbershop man turning away,
sides of his face
lathered and shaved
close with the cut-throat
he always uses,

big barbershop man turning away,
helping the neighbours
make good, sweating
inside a stretched t-shirt
with NO MEANS YES on the back of it,

waltzing a side of pig,
taking the weight,
scalp like a glove
rucked with the strain,
big barbershop man turning away
trim inside like a slice of ham

big barbershop man
hoisting the forequarter,
fat marbled with meat
stiff as a wardrobe,

big barbershop man
waltzing a side of pig
striped like a piece
of sun awning, cool
as a jelly roll,
big barbershop man waltzing the meat
like a barber's pole on yellow Main Street.

The dry well

It was not always a dry well.
Once it had been brimming with water.
cool, limpid, delicious water,
but a man came and took water from the well
and a woman came and took water from the well
and a man took water from the well again

>   and the well could not drink
>   from the low, slack water-table.

The well lacked a sense of its own danger
and a man came to take water from the well
and a woman came to take water from the well

>   but as the man was coming again
>   the well sighed in the dry darkness,
>   the well spoke in a quiet voice
>   from the deep-down bell of its emptiness
>   *Give me some water.*

But the man was at work with his heavy bucket
and he cried cheerfully, *Wait half a minute,*
I will just draw one more bucketful!

When he swung it up it was full of dust
and he was angry with the well.
Could it not have held out longer?
He had only needed one more bucketful.

Heron

It's evening on the river,
steady, milk-warm,

the nettles head-down
with feasting caterpillars,

the current turning,
thin as a blade-bone.

Reed-mace shivers.
I'm miles from anywhere.

Who's looking?
did a fish jump?

– and then a heron goes up
from its place by the willow.

With ballooning flight
it picks up the sky

and makes off, loaded.
I wasn't looking,

I heard the noise of its wings
and I turned,

I thought of a friend,
a cool one with binoculars,

here's rarity
with big wing-flaps, suiting itself.

One yellow chicken

One yellow chicken
she picks up expertly and not untenderly
from the conveyor of chickens.

Its soft beak gobbles feverishly
at a clear liquid which might be
a dose of sugar-drenched serum –

the beak's flexible membrane
seems to engulf the chicken
as it tries to fix on the dropper's glass tip.

Clear yellow juice gulps through a tube
and a few drops, suddenly colourless,
swill round a gape wide as the brim of a glass

but the chicken doesn't seem afraid –
or only this much, only for this long
until the lab assistant flicks it back on
to the slowly moving conveyor of chickens
and it tumbles, catches itself,
then buoyed up by the rest
reels out of sight, cheeping.

Sailing to Cuba

I'd climbed the crab-apple in the wind
that wild season of Cuba,

I leaned out on the twigs
to where clouds heeled over like sails
on the house-bounded horizon,

but even from here I felt the radio throb
like someone who was there when the accident happened
'not two yards from where I was standing',

then Big Band music cha-cha'd from room to room
to fill in time between news.

At school we learned 'Quinquireme of Nineveh
from distant Ophir…' The ships nudged closer.
The wind roared to itself like applause.

Off the West Pier

Dropped yolks of shore-lamp quiver on tarmac –
the night's disturbed and the sea itself
sidles about after its storm, buttery,
melting along the groynes.

The sea's a martinet with itself,
will come this far and no farther
like a Prussian governess
corrupted by white sugar –

Oh but the stealth
with which it twitches aside mortar
and licks, and licks
moist grains off the shore.

By day it simply keeps marching
beat after beat like waves of soldiers
timed to the first push. In step with the music
it swells greenness and greyness, spills foam
onto a fly-swarming tide-line –
beertabs and dropped King Cones,
flotsam of inopportune partners
sticky with what came after.

A man lies on his back
settled along the swell, his knees
glimmering, catching a lick of moonlight,
lazy as a seagull on Christmas morning –
He should have greased himself with whale-blubber
like a twelve-year-old Goddess-chested
cross-Channel swimmer.
His sadness stripes through him like ink
leaving no space or him.
He paws slow arm sweeps and rolls
where the sea shoulders him.

Up there an aeroplane falters,
its red landing-lights on
scouting the coast home.
The pilot smokes a cigarette.
Its tip winks with each breath.

Winter 1955

We're strung out on the plain's upthrust,
bubbles against the sill of the horizon.
Already the dark folds each figure to itself
like a mother putting on her child's overcoat,
or a paid attendant, who quickly and deftly
slots goose-pimpled arms into their stoles.

My own mother is attending to her daughters
in the Christmas gloom of our long garden
before the others are born.
A stream's tongue takes its first courses:
in siren suits and our cheek-hugging bonnets
we put one foot each in that water.

Now standstill clumps sink and disappear
over the plate-edge of the world.
The trees hold up fingers like candelabra,
blue and unsure as the word 'distant'.
Casually heeled there, we circle
the New Look skirts of our mother.

The attendant's hands skim on a breast
fused into party-going ramparts of taffeta,
but he takes up his gaze into the hall
as if there's nothing to be sorry or glad for,
and nothing in the snowy eternity
that feathers his keyhole.

Rinsing

In the corded hollows of the wood
leaves fall.
How light it is.
The trees are rinsing themselves of leaves
like Degas laundresses, their forearms
cold with the jelly-smooth
blue of starch-water.

The laundresses lean back and yawn
with their arms still in the water
like beech-boughs, pliant
on leavings of air.

In the corded hollows of the wood
how light it is.
How my excitement
burns in the chamber.

To Betty, swimming

You're breast-up in the bubbling spaces you make for yourself,
your head in the air, pointy, demure,
ridiculous in its petalled swim-cap.

You chug slowly across the pool.
Your legs trail. Your arms won't sweep
more than a third of the full stroke,

yet when you look up you're curling with smiles,
complicit as if splashed
with mile-deep dives from the cliff's height.

In Berber's Ice Cream Parlour

A fat young man in BERBER'S ICE CREAM PARLOUR
under a tiled ceiling the colour of farm butter
with a mirror at 45° to his jaw.

His moist jowls, lucent and young
as the tuck where a baby's buttock and thigh join,
quiver a little, preparing
to meet the order he's given.

A tall glass skims the waitress's breasts.
He holds on, spoon poised
to see if the syrup'll trickle right

past the mound of chopped nuts to the ice-
white luscious vanilla sheltering
under its blanket of cream.

The yellow skin weakens and melts.
He devotes himself,
purses his lips to wrinkling-point,

digs down with the long spoon
past jelly and fruit
to the depths, with the cool
inching of an expert.

Beside him there's a landscape in drained pink
and blue suggesting the sea
with an audacious cartoon economy.
They've even put in one white triangle
to make the horizon. A sail.

Large creamy girls mark the banana splits
with curls and squiggles,
pour sauce on peach melbas,
thumb in real strawberries.

Their bodies sail behind the counters,
balloons tight at the ropes, held down
by a customer's need for more clotted cream
topping on his three-tier chocolate sundae.

They have eight tables to serve.
With their left hands they slap out the change
and comets smelling of nickel
for kids' take-away treats,

and over on the bar counter there's room
for adult, luxurious absorption
of dark mocha ice cream.

Flowing, damp-curled, the waitresses
pass with their trays
doubled by mirrors, bumping like clouds.

Not going to the forest

If you had said the words 'to the forest'
at once I would have gone there
leaving my garden of broccoli and potato-plants.

I would not have struggled

to see the last ribbons of daylight
and windy sky tear over the crowns
of the oaks which stand here,
heavy draught animals
bearing, continually bearing.

I would have rubbed the velvety forest
against my cheek like the pincushion
I sewed with invisible stitches.

No. But you said nothing
and I have a child to think of
and a garden of parsnips and raspberries.
It's not that I'm afraid,
but that I'm still gathering
the echoes of my five senses –

how far they've come with me, how far
they want to go on.

So the whale-back of the forest
shows for an instant, then dives.
I think it has oxygen within it
to live, downward, for miles.

Lutherans

Whichever way I turned on the radio
there was Sibelius
or an exceptionally long weather forecast.
Good practice: I'd purse up my lips
to the brief gulp of each phrase.

Sometimes I struck a chord with the World Service's
sense-fuzz, like the smell of gardenia
perfume in Woolworth's: instantly cloying,
the kind that doesn't bloom on your skin,

or, in the two p.m. gloom of the town square,
I'd catch the pale flap of a poster
for the Helsingin Sanomat: POMPIDOU KUOLLUT.
I'd buy one, but never wrestle beyond the headline.

When pupils asked what I thought of 'this three-day week'
I'd mention the candle-blaze
nightly in my room during the power-cuts,
and the bronchitis I had,
but I'd balance the fact that I smoked too much
against the marsh-chill when the heating went off.

I'd always stop on the railway bridge
even at one in the morning. The city was shapeless, squeezed in
by hills bristling with Sitka spruce.
The drunks had their fires lit
but they were slow, vulnerable, frozen
while flaming on a half-litre from the State Alcohol Shop.

If their luck held they'd bunch on the Sports Hall heating-grates
rather than be chipped free from a snow heap
in the first light of ten in the morning,
among a confusion of fur-hatted burghers
going to have coffee and cakes.
Work started at eight, there was never enough time.
They'd stop, chagrined, and murmur 'It's shocking'.

They were slowly learning not to buy the full-cream milk
of their farming childhoods; there was a government campaign
with leaflets on heart disease and exercise
and a broadsheet on the energy crisis
with diagrams suggesting the angles
beyond which windows should never be opened.

Their young might be trim, but they kept
a pious weakness for sinning on cake
and for those cloudy, strokeable hats
that frame Lutheran pallor.
After an evening visit to gym, they'd roll
the green cocoon of their ski-suited baby
onto the pupils' table. Steadied with one hand
it lay prone and was never unpacked.

FROM

RECOVERING A BODY

(1994)

To Virgil

Lead me with your cold, sure hand,
make me press the correct buttons
on the automatic ticket machine,
make me not present my ticket upside down
to the slit mouth at the barriers,

then make the lift not jam
in the hot dark of the deepest lines.
May I hear the voice on the loudspeaker
and understand each syllable
of the doggerel of stations.

If it is rush-hour, let me be close to the doors,
I do not ask for space,
let no one crush me into a corner
or accidentally squeeze hard on my breasts
or hit me with bags or chew gum in my face.

If there are incidents, let them be over,
let there be no red-and-white tape
marking the place, make it not happen
when the tunnel has wrapped its arms around my train
and the lights have failed.

Float me up the narrow escalator
not looking backward, losing my balance
or letting go of your cold, sure hand.
Let there not be a fire
in the gaps, hold me secure.
Let me come home to the air.

Three Ways of Recovering a Body

By chance I was alone in my bed the morning
I woke to find my body had gone.
It had been coming. I'd cut off my hair in sections
so each of you would have something to remember,
then my nails worked loose from their beds
of oystery flesh. Who was it got them?
One night I slipped out of my skin. It lolloped
hooked to my heels, hurting. I had to spray on
more scent so you could find me in the dark,
I was going so fast. One of you begged for my ears
because you could hear the sea in them.

First I planned to steal myself back. I was a mist
on thighs, belly and hips. I'd slept with so many men.
I was with you in the ash-haunted stations of Poland,
I was with you on that grey plaza in Berlin
while you wolfed three doughnuts without stopping,
thinking yourself alone. Soon I recovered my lips
by waiting behind the mirror while you shaved.
You pouted. I peeled away kisses like wax
no longer warm to the touch. Then I flew off.

Next I decided to become a virgin. Without a body
it was easy to make up a new story. In seven years
every invisible cell would be renewed
and none of them would have touched any of you.
I went to a cold lake, to a grey-lichened island,
I was gold in the wallet of the water.
I was known to the inhabitants, who were in love
with the coveted whisper of my virginity:
all too soon they were bringing me coffee and perfume,
cash under stones. I could really do something for them.

Thirdly I tried marriage to a good husband
who knew my past but forgave it. I believed in the power
of his penis to smoke out all those men
so that bit by bit my body service would resume,
although for a while I'd be the one woman in the world
who was only present in the smile of her vagina.
He stroked the air where I might have been.
I turned to the mirror and saw mist gather
as if someone lived in the glass. Recovering
I breathed to myself, *'Hold on! I'm coming.'*

Holiday to Lonely

He's going on holiday to lonely
but no one knows. He has got the sunblock
the cash and the baseball cap
shorts that looked nice in the shop
then two days' indoor bicycling
to get his legs ready.

He plans to learn something in lonely.
Bits of the language, new dishes.
He would like to try out a sport –
jet-ski maybe, or fishing.
You are meant to be alone, fishing.
There are books about it at the airport.

In the departure lounge, he has three hours
to learn to harpoon a marlin
and to overhear the history
of that couple quarrelling
about Bourbon and Jamesons –
which is the best way to have fun.

He is starting to like the look of lonely
with its steady climate, its goals
anyone can touch. He settles
for drinking lots of Aqua Libra
and being glad about Airmiles
as the Australian across the aisle
plugs into *Who's That Girl?*

Poem in a Hotel

Waiting. I'm here waiting
like a cable-car caught in a thunderstorm.
At six someone will feed me, at seven
I'll stroll and sit by the band.

I have never seen so many trombones
taking the air, or so many mountains.
Under them there are tunnels
to a troll's salt-garden.

The lake is a dirty thumb-mark.
If nowhere has a middle
this lake is its navel,
pregnant with sickeningly large carp.

Bent as if travelling backwards, the birches
wipe the cheeks of 29 parasols.
A little girl scythes at her shuttlecock:
4, 6, 7 strokes –

there are 29 bright parasols
outfacing the sun
and the little girl wears a red cap
to blunt her vision.

I lie through half a morning
with my eyelids gummed down,
neither rising nor falling
until the next meal comes round.

I keep a straw in my mouth
so I can breathe,
I am drinking Sprite in a hotel,
I am a carp in the reeds.

The Bike Lane

Of course they're dead, or this is a film.
Along the promenade the sun
moves down council-painted white lanes –

these are for cycling. On the other hand
the sea is going quietly out to France,
taking its time. If the cliffs are white,

iron stanchions are planted in them
so a bleed of rust can be seen
by the army rafting its way in

on lilos and pedalos. Professional cyclists
walk with one hand on the saddle,
waiting to be told to put on

red vests which show up in the race.
The aisle of the falling tide
squints to infinity, the bike-lane

is much in need of repainting
like the smile of the sea-front towards France.
In the less-than-shelter of the beach huts

two people I love are waiting
with as much infinity in their laps
as you can catch with a red vest on.

The cyclists flash past them –
one turns his keyed-up white face
but they are dead and this is a film.

Drink and the Devil

On his skin the stink
of last night turned
to acetaldehyde.
What comes through the curtains must be light.
It combs the shadows of his brain
and frightens him.

Things not to think of crowd in.
The things she said
as if sick of saying them.
The jumpy blanks in what happened.
The way he skidded and there
was the kid looking,

staring through the bars of the landing
so I shouted *Monkey, Monkey*
and danced but he wouldn't laugh.
Or was that in the club?
I would never harm a hair
on the head of him.
If she doesn't know that she knows nothing.

Ahvenanmaa

Breast to breast against the azaleas
they pitch, father and daughter,

the sun throws itself down
golden, glittering,

pale orange petals clutter their hair
as he catches her shoulders,

braced, they grapple and bruise
among the perfumed azaleas.

The flowers loll out their tongues,
tigers on dark stems

while breast to breast against the azaleas
they pitch, father and daughter.

The ferry slides between islands.
Pale and immediate, the sun rises.

The hull noses white marker-posts
glittering in summer water –

here, now, the channel deepens,
the sky darkens. Too cold in her dress

the girl scutters. Engine vents veil
steam while rain hides Ahvenanmaa.

Rubbing Down the Horse

The thing about a saddle is that second
you see it so closely, sweat-grains
pointing the leather,
pulled stitching and all, and the pommel gone black
and reins wrapped over themselves.
You see it so closely
because you have one foot in the stirrup
and someone else has your heel in his hand.
Your heel in someone else's hand

that second before they lift you, your face
turned to the saddle, the sweat marks
and smell of the horse, those stitches pulling
the way they tug and tear in your flesh
when you lie there in pain,
the hooves of it cutting,
trying to pin down the place, the time.
The nurse has your heel in her hand
yellow and still, already tender
though on Friday you were walking.

She is taking a pinprick
or else slowly, bit by bit, washing
your wrapped body from the heels upward
and talking, always talking.
She might want to ask someone
what way you would move when sunlight
filled the cobbles like straw,
or how without looking at it
you'd kick in place a zinc bucket
then bend and rub down the horse.

You came back to life in its sweetness

You came back to life in its sweetness,
to keen articulations of the knee joint,
to slow replays of balls kicking home
and the gape of the goalkeeper.

You came back to life in its sweetness,
to the smell of sweat, the night-blue
unwrinkling of the iris,
and going from table to table at parties.

Perhaps you'll waltz
on some far-off anniversary
with an elderly woman
who doesn't exist yet,

and you, you'll forget,
for now we're counting in years,
where we were counting in hours.

Heimat

Deep in busy lizzies and black iron
he sleeps for the Heimat,
and his photograph slips in and out of sight
as if breathing.

There are petals against his cheeks
but he is not handsome.
His small eyes search the graveyard fretfully
and the flesh of his cheeks clouds
the bones of heroism.

No one can stop him being young
and he is so tired of being young.
He would like to feel pain in his joints
as he wanders down to Hübers,
but he's here as always,
always on his way back from the photographer's
in his army collar
with a welt on his neck rubbed raw.

The mountains are white and sly as they always were.
Old women feed the graveyard with flowers,
clear the glass on his photograph
with chamois leathers,
bend and whisper the inscription.
They are his terrible suitors.

In the Desert Knowing Nothing

Here I am in the desert knowing nothing,
here I am knowing nothing
in the desert of knowing nothing,
here I am in this wide
desert long after midnight

here I am knowing nothing
hearing the noise of the rain
and the melt of fat in the pan

here is our man on the phone knowing something
and here's our man fresh from the briefing
in combat jeans and a clip microphone
testing for sound,
catching the desert rain, knowing something,

here's the general who's good with his men
storming the camera, knowing something
in the pit of his Americanness
here's the general taut in his battledress
and knowing something

here's the boy washing his kit in a tarpaulin
on a front-line he knows from his GCSE
coursework on Wilfred Owen
and knowing something

here is the plane banking,
the *go go go* of adrenalin
the child melting
and here's the grass that grows overnight
from the desert rain, feeling for him
and knowing everything

and here I am knowing nothing
in the desert of knowing nothing
dry from not speaking.

Poem on the Obliteration of 100,000 Iraqi Soldiers

They are hiding away in the desert,
hiding in sand which is growing warm
with the hot season,

they are hiding from bone-wagons
and troops in protective clothing
who will not look at them,

the crowds were appalled on seeing him,
so disfigured did he look
that he seemed no longer human.

That killed head straining through the windscreen
with its frill of bubbles in the eye-sockets
is not trying to tell you something –

it is telling you something.
Do not look away,
permit them, permit them –

they are telling their names to the Marines
in one hundred thousand variations,
but no one is counting,

do not turn away,

for God is counting
all of us who are silent
holding our newspapers up, hiding.

The Yellow Sky

That morning when the potato tops rusted,
the mangle rested and the well ran dry
and the turf house leaned like a pumpkin
against the yellow sky

there was a fire lit in the turf house
and a thin noise of crying,
and under the skinny sheets a woman
wadded with cloth against bleeding.

That morning her man went to the fields
after a shy pause at the end of her bed,
trying not to pick out the smell of her blood,
but she turned and was quiet.

All day the yellow sky walked on the turves
and she thought of things heavy to handle,
her dreams sweated with burdens,
the bump and grind of her mangle.

All day the child creaked in her cradle
like a fire as it sinks
and the woman crooned when she was able
across the impossible inches.

At that moment at the horizon there came a horseman
pressed to the saddle, galloping, galloping
fast as the whoop of an ambulance siren –
and just as unlikely. What happened

was slower and all of a piece.
She died. He lived (the man in the fields),
the child got by on a crust
and lived to be thirty, with sons. In the end
we came to be born too. Just.

Getting the Strap

The Our Father, the moment of fear.
He dodged round us and ran,
but was fetched back again
to stand before us on the platform.

The Our Father, the moment of fear
as the fist gripped and he hung
from the headmaster's arm,
doubling on the spot like a rabbit
blind for home.

The Our Father, the moment of fear.
The watch he'd stolen was given
back to its owner, dumb
in the front row, watching the strapping.

The Our Father, the moment of fear.
The strap was old and black and it cracked
on belly buttock and once across his lip
because he writhed and twisted.
He would not stand and take it.

The Our Father, the moment of fear.
There was a lot of sun
leaking through churchy windows
onto a spurt of urine.
After an age of watching
we sang the last hymn.

Adders

This path is silky with dust
where a lizard balances across bracken fronds
and a brown butterfly opens wide
to the stroke of the sun,

where a trawler feels its way along the sandbanks
and two yachts, helplessly paired, tack far out
like the butterflies which have separated and gone quiet.

A wild damson tree bulges with wasps
among heaps that are not worth picking,
and there a branch splits white with the lightning
of too heavy a harvest.

The lizard is gone in a blink.
Its two-pronged tail – half withered, half growing –
flicks out of the sun.
For a moment the pulse in its throat
keeps the grass moving.

A grass-bound offering of yarrow,
rosebay willow herb and veined convolvulus
lies to one side of the path
as if someone's coming back.
Instead, the sift of the dust –
beneath the bracken these hills are full of adders.

The conception

In the white sheets I gave you
everything I am capable of –
at the wrong time
of the month we opened
to the conception,

you were dewed like a plum
when at two a.m.
you reached under the bed
for a drink of water adrift
in yesterday's clothes,

our sheets were a rope
caught between our thighs,
we might easily have died
but we kept on climbing.

Scan at 8 weeks

The white receiver
slides up my vagina,

I turn and you've come,
though I'm much too old for this
and you're much too young.

That's the baby
says the radiographer.
You are eight millimetres long
and pulsing,

bright in the centre of my much-used womb
which to my astonishment
still looks immaculate.

You are all heart,
I watch you tick and tick

and wonder
what you will come to,

will this be our only encounter
in the white gallery of ultrasound

or are you staying?
One day will we talk about this

moment when I first saw your spaceship
far off, heading for home?

Pedalo

She swam to me smiling, her teeth
pointed by salt water, her mouth

a rock-pool's spat-out wine gum,
and then the tide flung

over her threshold,
and her lips moved.

The valve of her mouth was plumed
with salt-sweet tendrils,

sea danced from her pelt
of oil and muscle,

she rested her elbows on my pedalo
and there she hung

browning the pads of her shoulders
like a snake in the sun.

On shore thunderhead pines
drifted and swelled
like August umbrellas
stunning the fronts of hotels.

The sharp tide rinsed
over her threshold
as she dived once
and an angler cast
with lightning-proof rod
from the crinkled rocks.

A slow Medusa tilted beneath her,
shadowing toes and ankles
then on with its belly to the south,
braille on its tentacles.
She could read it like a newspaper
as it hunted alongside her.

I shivered
at the roll of her syllables,
and her joined feet winnowing,

and so I trawled her with me
over a shallow forest of dog-jawed
fruit sucking the trees,

past angler-fish socketing sand
with stone-cold faces,
through shrimps which divided between them
her armpit crevices

then flicked that way and this
tasting the dew of her breasts.

I trawled her past innocent sand
and the spumy outstretched arms
of agar and tangle –
but no, I wouldn't look down

however she called to me
until my fingers were shrunk
like old laundry.

I did not dare look down
to be snagged by ruby and seal-black
trees relaxing their weave.

On shore nobody's waiting.
The children, firm and delicious
as morning goods, have sheathed up their spades.

The boy with burned legs
has stepped out of his pantaloons
and skips in his blue vest
on the verandah boards.

The big one lights a mosquito candle,
Dad fills his glass of wine
four times, while they count,

and crickets saw in the ditch, frantic
along with the old car number-plate
and the boys' jar of fishing maggots.

They are screeching, all of them:
night, night, night's come
and no one's ever had a pedalo out this long.

Night-wind sifts on the shore
where striped recliners and wind-breaks
squeak by the green pavilion
crying for more.

I've lost my wife to the sea
Dad thinks hazily,
and takes another bottle of Muscadet
out of the gas cooler,

he imagines her dreaming
and sleeping miles from him,

each breath takes her farther,
toes in the air,

sea claps under her pedalo
impudently happy –

Below me now a mirror of wave-ruts
in firm brown sand,
I'd pulled her with me for miles
and there was nowhere to hide.

Now let me see you swim back
I said. She was mouthing
like mackerel tossed in a bucket
when the man's too busy to kill it,

with her scale-lapped bathing-hat
fly-blown and crazing.
She had nothing on underneath.
She was bare and bald as an eel.

  Now she was an old bathing-woman
  a mackintoshed marine Venus,
  now she was that girl with lipstick
  a push-up bra and a beehive,

  now she was a slippery customer at Cannes
  bare-breasted and young,
  now she was my old
  familiar snake again.

I took her curls in my hands and I pulled
but they were limpetted, smiling,
and there were just the two of us rocking.

We were close as spies
and she stayed silent
till day dived after its horizon
and the sea rustled with moonlight.

Swell shuts and opens
like a throat,

she claps
under my pedalo
impudently happy.

Where are you now
my sister, my spouse?

Clap with one hand
or clap to nothing –
I know you can.

Kiss me with the kisses of your mouth
my sister, my spouse.

The pedalo rocks
and is still again.

Beetroot Soup

Its big red body ungulps
from the bowl in the fridge
with a fat shiver.

Glazed
with yellow beading of grease
the soup melts from the edge,

yesterday's beetroot
turns the texture of tongues
rolling their perfect ovals
out of the silt at the bottom.

Like duck breast-feathers, the dumplings
wisp to the surface, curl
as the soup brightens
just off the boil.

There'll be pearl onions
– two to a mouthful –
white butter,
then later

plums
piled in a bucket
under the table
thatched with dull leaves
and a black
webbing of twig
over their round
sleep.

When the soup's done
yellow
constellations
burst on its skin,

bread goes to work
wiping and sopping

the star-scum
set in a slick

on the base of the pot –
chicken fat.

The Diving Reflex

Where the great ship sank I am,
where cathedrals of ice breathe through me
down naves of cold
I tread and roll,

where the light goes
and the pressure weighs
in the rotten caves of an iceberg's side
I glide,

I am mute, not breathing,
my shoulders hunched to the stream
with the whales, drowsing.

Bells rang in my blood
as I went down
purling, heart over heel
through the nonchalant
fish–clad ocean –

her inquisitive kiss
slowed me to this
great cartwheel.

Down I go, tied to my rope.
I have my diving reflex to sister me,
and the blubbery sea cow
nods, knowing me.

There is blood in my veins
too thick for panic,
there is a down
so deep a whale
thins to a sheet of paper
and here I hang.
I will not drown.

*The diving reflex can enable the human body to shut down and maintain
life for as long as forty minutes underwater at low temperatures.*

Bathing at Balnacarry

Two miles or so beyond
the grey flank of the farm
and the wall of gravestones
the oncoming rain
put an edge on the mountains,

they were blue and sure
as the blade of a pocket knife
whizzed to a razor traverse
cutting the first
joint of my thumb –

It was stitched, not bleeding,
the dark threads in the sea were weeds
and my son was packing them
between the stones of his dam.

He was holding back the river
while the mountain punctured clouds
to hold back rain
no farther off than we'd cycled
bumping towards our swim.

In the grey purse of Balnacarry
there were red pebbles and smooth pebbles
and the close grain of the water,

the men were absent –
one walking in the woods
one fishing off the rocks –

the child behind me built up his dam
through which the downpour would blossom
in the sea at Balnacarry –
it was cold, but not lonely
as I stripped and swam.

Boys on the Top Board

Boys on the top board
too high to catch.
Noon is painting them out.

Where the willow swans
on the quarry edge
they tan and sweat

in the place of divers
with covered nipples –
Olympians,

that was the way of it.
Boys in the breeze
on the top board

where the willow burns
golden and green
on feet grappling –

boys fooling
shoulder to shoulder,
light shaking.

The lake's in shadow,
the day's cooling,
time to come down –

they stub their heels on the sun
then pike-dive
out of its palm.

Sylvette Scrubbing

Sylvette scrubbing,
arms of a woman
marbled with muscle
swabbing the sill,

tiny red grains
like suck kisses
on Sylvette's skin,
Sylvette's wrists
in and out of the water
as often as otters.

She grips that pig of a brush
squirts bristle
makes the soap crawl then
wipes it all up.

Babes in the Wood

Father,
I remember when you left us.
I knew all along
it was going to happen.
You gave me bread but wouldn't look at me
and Hansel couldn't believe it
because you were his hero,
but I loved you and knew
when you stroked my hair you were bound to leave us.

It was Hansel who crumbled the bread
while I skipped at your side and pretended
to prattle questions and guess nothing.

Father,
did you drive home quickly or slowly,
thinking of your second family
waiting to grab your legs with shrieks of *'Daddy!'*
and of your new wife's face, smoothing
now she sees you're alone?

Father,
we love it here in the forest.
Hansel's got over it. I've learned to fish
and shoot rabbits with home-made arrows.
We've even built ourselves a house
where the wolves can't get us.
But wolves don't frighten us much
even when they howl in the dark.
With wolves, you know where you are.

Cajun

This is what I want –

to be back again
with the night to come –

slipper-bags across our saddles
how fast we rode
and all for nothing.

Your lips on his lips
your hand in his hand
as you went from the dance.

We heard Mass at dawn,
When I knelt for communion

it was the hem of your white dress
I felt in my mouth,

it was your lips moving.

This is all I want

to be there again
with the night to come –

meet me where the fire
lights the bayou

watch my sweat shine
as I play for you.

It is for you I play
my voice leaping the flames,

if you don't come
I am nothing.

Skips

If I wanted totems, in place of the poles
slung up by barbers, in place of the clutter
of knife-eyed kids playing with tops and whips,
and boys in cut-down men's trousers
swaggering into camera,
I'd have skips.

First, red and white bollards
to mark the road-space they need.
A young couple in stained workwear
– both clearly solicitors –
act tough with the driver, who's late.
The yellow god with its clangorous emptiness
sways on the chains.
The young man keeps shouting *BACK A LITTLE!*
as the skip rides above his BMW.
The driver, vengeful, drops it askew.

Next, the night is alive with neighbours
bearing their gifts, propitiations
and household gods – a single-tub washing-machine,
a cat-pissed rug, two televisions.
Soundless as puppets, they lower them
baffled in newspaper, then score
a dumbshow goal-dance to the corner.

Time by Accurist

Washed silk jacket by Mesa
in cream or taupe, to order,
split skirt in lime
from a selection at Cardoon,
£84.99,
lycra and silk body, model's own,
calf-skin belt by Bondage, £73.99,
tights from a range at Pins,
deck-shoes, white, black or strawberry,
all from Yoo Hoo,
baby's cotton trousers and braces
both at Workaday
£96.00; see list for stockists.

Photographs by André McNair,
styled by Lee LeMoin,
make-up by Suze Fernando at Face the Future,
hair by Joaquim for Plumes.
Models: Max and Claudie.
Location: St James Street Washeteria
(courtesy of Route Real America
and the Cape Regis Hotel),

baby, model's own,
lighting by Sol,
time by Accurist.

The Silent Man in Waterstones

I shall be the first to lead the Muses to my native land
VIRGIL

The silent man in Waterstones
LOVE on one set of knuckles
HATE on the other
JESUS between his eyes
drives his bristling blue skull
into the shelves,
thuds on CRIME / FANTASY
shivers a stand of Virago Classics
head-butts Dante.

The silent man in Waterstones
looks for a bargain.
Tattered in flapping parka
white eyes wheeling
he catches
light on his bloody earlobes
and on the bull-ring
he wears through his nose.

The silent man in Waterstones
raps for attention.
He has got Virgil by the ears:
primus ego in patriam mecum...
He'll lead the Muse to a rat-pissed underpass
teach her to beg
on a carpet of cardboard
and carrier bags.

The Wardrobe Mistress

This is the wardrobe mistress, touching
her wooden wardrobe. Here is her smokey
cross of chrysanthemums
skewed by the font.

They have put you in this quietness
left you here for the night.
Your coffin is like a locker
of mended ballet shoes.

You always looked in the toes.
There was blood in them, rusty
as leaves, blood from ballerinas.
Tonight it is All Souls

but you'll stop here quietly,
only the living have gone to the cemetery
candles in their hands
to be blown about under the Leylandii.

In your wooden wardrobe, you're used to waiting.
You know these sounds to the bone:
they are showing people to their seats
tying costumes at the back.

Everything they say is muffled,
the way it is backstage.
A stagehand pushes your castors
so you glide forward.

You know Manon is leaning
on points against a flat,
nervously flexing
her strong, injured feet,

you're in position too, arms crossed,
touching your bud of wood.
You needn't dance, it's enough
to do what you always did.

That was the second bell. You feel it
tang through the crush. The wind
pours on like music
drying everyone's lips,

they're coming, your dancers.
You hate the moment of hush.
There. The quick luck-words
knocking on wood.

When You've Got

When you've got the plan of your life
matched to the time it will take
but you just want to press SHIFT / BREAK
and print over and over
this is not what I was after
this is not what I was after,

when you've finally stripped out the house
with its iron-cold fireplace,
its mouldings, its mortgage,
its single-skin walls
but you want to write in the plaster
'This is not what I was after,'

when you've got the rainbow-clad baby
in his state-of-the-art pushchair
but he arches his back at you
and pulps his Activity Centre
and you just want to whisper
'This is not what I was after,'

when the vacuum seethes and whines in the lounge
and the waste-disposal unit blows,
when tenners settle in your account
like snow hitting a stove,
when you get a chat from your spouse
about marriage and personal growth,

when a wino comes to sleep in your porch
on your Citizen's Charter
and you know a hostel's opening soon
but your headache's closer
and you really just want to torch
the bundle of rags and newspaper

and you'll say to the newspaper
'This is not what we were after,
this is not what we were after.'

BESTIARY

　　　　　　　　　...I was at home
And should have been most happy, – but I saw
Too far into the sea, where every maw
The greater on the less feeds evermore. –
But I saw too distinct into the core
Of an eternal fierce destruction,
And so from happiness I far was gone.
Still am I sick of it, and tho', to-day,
I've gather'd young spring-leaves, and flowers gay
Of periwinkle and wild strawberry,
Still do I that most fierce destruction see, –
The Shark at savage prey, – the Hawk at pounce, –
The gentle Robin, like a Pard or Ounce,
Ravening a worm...

JOHN KEATS
Epistle to John Hamilton Reynolds

Candle poem
(after Sa'di Yusuf)

A candle for the ship's breakfast
eaten while moving southward
through mild grey water
with the work all done,
a candle for the house seen from outside,
the voices and shadows
of the moment before coming home,

a candle for the noise of aeroplanes
going elsewhere, passing over,
for delayed departures, embarrassed silences
between people who love one another,
a candle for sandwiches in service stations
at four a.m., and the taste of coffee
from plastic cups, thickened with sugar
to keep us going,

a candle for the crowd around a coffin
and the terrible depth it has to fall
into the grave dug for everyone,
the deaths for decades to come,
our deaths; a candle for going home
and feeling hungry after saying
we would never be able to eat the ham,
the fruit cake, those carefully-buttered buns.

At the Emporium

He is the one you can count on
for yesterday's bread, rolling tobacco
and the staccato
tick of the blinds
on leathery Wednesday afternoons.
He has hand-chalked boards with the prices
of Anchor butter and British wine.
He doesn't hold with half-day closing.

He's the king of long afternoons
lounging vested in his doorway.
He watches the children dwindle
and dawdle, licking icepops
that drip on the steps.
His would be the last face that saw them
before an abduction. Come in,
he is always open.

Next door

is the same as ours, but different.
Back to front stairs, and a bass that thuds
like the music of demolition
year after year, but the house
is still standing.

When we have parties they tense into silence,
though they are good at fighting.
After the last screech and slam, their children
play war on their scab of a lawn.

We are mirrors of one another,
never showing what's real.
If I turn like this, quickly,
and look over the fence, what will I see?

He lived next door all his life

One year he painted his front door yellow.
It was the splash of a carrier bag
in the dun terrace,
but for the rest he was inconspicuous.

He went out one way and came back the other,
often carrying laundry and once compost
for the tree he thought might do in the back yard.
Some time later there was its skeleton
taking up most of the bin.

He passed the remark 'It's a pity'
when it rained on a Saturday,
and of a neighbour's child he said 'terror'.
He picked his words like scones from a plate,

dropping no crumbs. When his front door shut
he was more gone than last Christmas.
But for the girls stored in his cellar
to learn what it meant
to have no pity, to be terror,
he was there.

The surgeon husband

Here at my worktop, foil-wrapping a silver salmon
– yes, a whole salmon – I'm thinking
of the many bodies of women
that my husband daily opens.

Here he lunges at me in wellingtons.
He is up to his armpits, a fisherman
tugging against the strength of the current.

I imagine the light for him, clean,
and a green robing of willow
and the fish hammering upstream.

I too tug at the flaps of the salmon
where its belly was, trying to straighten
the silver seams before they are sewn.
We are one in our dreams.

The epidural is patchy, his assistant's
handwriting is slipping. At eleven fifteen
they barb their patient to sleep, jot 'knife to skin',
and the nurse smiles over her mask at the surgeon.

But I am quietly dusting out the fish-kettle,
and I have the salmon clean as a baby
grinning at me from the table.

Fishing beyond sunset

The boy in the boat, the tip of the pole,
slow swing of the boat as the wash goes round
from other boats with lights on, heading home
to islands, from islands: anyway they come.

Thirty-four bass, small bass, not worth keeping.
See them in the water, the hang
of twice-caught fish playing dumb,
then the shake-off of air. The kickdown

always surprises you, makes your feet grip
on the planks of the boat. There is the line
disappearing into the sunset
or so it seems, but it is plumbed

by your finger, which sees nothing
but a breeze of line running through water.
Behind you a sheet of fire
does something to pole, to boat, to boy.

Hare in the snow

Hare in the snow cresting
the run of winter, stretching
in liquid leaps over the hill,

then the wind turns, and
hare stands so still

he is a freeze of himself, fooling
the shadows into believing
he is one of them.

Need

(a version from Piers Plowman: *'The Pardon sent from Truth')*

I know that no one dare judge another's need,
for need is our neighbour, blood to our bone:
the prisoner in Long Lartin, the poor of shantytown
bearing children, burdened by bad landlords,
struggling to scrape together what goes straight out
on rent, on never enough food for the children
who cry like crickets from hunger, night-long.

They slave while they're sick with hunger,
wake in the damp of winter, crouch between wall and cradle
to rock the crying baby, their raw fingers
chapped with outworking, seaming denim
for half nothing, pitiful labour paid by the hour
which takes them nowhere, only to one more
half-hour's heat on the meter, scraping and struggling,
working for nothing.

The misery of women in run-down hostels
the misery of the men crammed in with them
racked by the nothing that is all they have,
too proud to beg, to show they are slowly starving
withering away, their poverty hidden like AIDS,
a shame that must never be shown to their neighbours
a shame that has made strangers of neighbours
and hunger the only guest at all their meals.

The world has kicked into me the future
of children born into poverty's welcome
to parents who have nothing but surplus labour,
empty hands, thoughts nobody wants.
Chips are their Sunday roast, dog-ends rolled up in Rizlas
damp down the parents' hunger as they look on
while the kids eat baked beans and bacon.
By the State's cold calculation
they could get by on carrots and bakers' leavings.
Only love can help them.

These will not beg, but there are beggars
who shoot up everything they're given
who have nothing at all wrong with them
who could perfectly well do a day's work
who deserve no pity, no money, nothing.
Even if they collapse on the streets, coughing
from the come-back of ancient diseases
think nothing of it. Don't be ashamed to walk past
with your wallet stuffed with credit cards
as the Bible says.

But yet. Look again. What about these beggars
who look perfectly all right, able to do a day's work,
ought to be cleared off the streets – all that? And yet
some of them come from another world, or another time.
Care in the community is the cold calculation
that takes care of them. Stop. Look again.
They live by the phases of the moon
by an inner fire that will not leave them alone.
They are penniless as time and tide, wander with nothing
like the holy apostles, Peter and Paul.
They have no time for preaching or miracles
but they can speak in tongues if you listen,
and catch the wind of truth in the sails
of what seems like play.

God who can do anything
might have made them businessmen,
but instead he made them his own children
and sent them out with empty bank accounts
holey jeans and a blanket to wrap around them.
These secret disciples break all the rules but his,
the one rule that tells us to love, and give.

Think. You will even put up with poets
for the sake of their patrons, if these are rich men,
publishers who fancy culture, and keep a newspaper.
Think of the Lord of heaven who has sent his children
to be called madmen, and please him
if you can, by throwing some cash at them.

And think again. When you are begging
for God's pardon, when the daylight after death
shines on your sins, think of them,
God's secret children, born pardoned,
and what you did for them.

Sometimes in the rough garden of city spaces

Sometimes in the rough garden of city spaces
where I believe a mugger will not approach me
because so far no mugger has approached me
I stop to take breath.
The city exists by acts of faith
that we and our children are safe,

that the pounding wheels of cars will miss them,
that the traffic will stop when the lights turn,
that parks will stay green, that money is not everything,
that the lime trees that line our streets are lopped and cropped
with the best of intentions,
that the orange glow of the streetlamps is moonlight
to that couple there, locked in each other, lost
in the city's night-time suspension.

I should like to be buried in a summer forest

I should like to be buried in a summer forest
where people go in July,
only a bus ride from the city,

I should like them to walk over me
not noticing anything but sunlight
and patches of wild strawberries –

Here! Look under the leaves!
I should like the child who is slowest
to end up picking the most,

and the big kids will show the little
the only way to grasp a nettle
and pick it so it doesn't sting.

I should like home-time to come
so late the bus has its lights on
and a cloud of moths hangs in their beam,

and when they are all gone
I should like to be buried in a summer forest
where the dark steps
blindfold, on cat foot-pads,
with the dawn almost touching it.

The scattering

First, the echo
at night, when I said
'I'll hold you'

and your voice like a bird's in the grey morning
came back 'Hold you',
and your feet in my palm
were barely hardened by walking,

and then the scattering,
the start of grammar
and distance.
You say, 'Hold me.'
You'll say, 'Don't hold me.'

All the things you are not yet
(for Tess)

Tonight there's a crowd in my head:
all the things you are not yet.
You are words without paper, pages
sighing in summer forests, gardens
where builders stub out their rubble
and plastic oozes its sweat.
All the things you are, you are not yet.

Not yet the lonely window in midwinter
with the whine of tea on an empty stomach,
not yet the heating you can't afford and must wait for,
tamping a coin in on each hour.
Not the gorgeous shush of restaurant doors
and their interiors, always so much smaller.
Not the smell of the newsprint, the blur
on your fingertips – your fame. Not yet

the love you will have for Winter Pearmains
and Chanel No.5 – and then your being unable
to buy both washing-machine and computer
when your baby's due to be born,
and my voice saying, 'I'll get you one'
and you frowning, frowning
at walls and surfaces which are not mine –
all this, not yet. Give me your hand,

that small one without a mark of work on it,
the one that's strange to the washing-up bowl
and doesn't know Fairy Liquid from whiskey.
Not yet the moment of your arrival in taxis
at daring destinations, or your being alone at stations
with the skirts of your fashionable clothes flapping
and no money for the telephone.

Not yet the moment when I can give you nothing
so well-folded it fits in an envelope –
a dull letter you won't reread.

Not yet the moment of your assimilation
in that river flowing westward: river of clothes,
of dreams, an accent unlike my own
saying to someone I don't know: *darling...*

Diving girl

She's next to nowhere, feeling no cold
in her white sluther of bubbles.
She comes to a point like a seal
in his deep dive, she is sleek.
As her nostrils close
she's at home. See how salt water slides
as she opens her eyes.

There is the word *naked*
but she's not spelled by it.
Look at her skin's steel glint
and the knife of her fins.
With the basking shark
with the minke whale
and the grey seal
she comes up to breathe
ten miles offshore.

A pretty shape

I never stop listening to you sing
long enough to know what I think.
All I do is let it go on.

The bubble of song bounces towards me
over the wet surfaces of the kitchen
and you with your arms folded
in that tiny immemorial way you've observed,
your soft, small arms folded
over your chest where your breath
flows and unflows easily,
don't need to look at me.
The bubble of your song bounces towards me
its surface tension strong
as it shudders, recovers.
You let the song go where it wants.

When you've fallen asleep, or I think you've fallen
I withdraw, still singing
or perhaps still listening to you sing,
but you feel me going. Why am I going
always going, instead of listening to you sing?
Your hand knows better than mine
and with authority
of touch I cannot match
wraps me round you again.

Viking cat in the dark

Viking cat in the dark
is paw-licked velvet, sinew of shadow,
a thread of smoke bitterly burning,
a quiver of black like a riddle.

The huts lie low
a hoard half-hidden
a clutch of eggs
in the dune's hollow

and horned helmets
are nightmares to wake from
shapes cut from dreams
– but the cat leaps.

Like rain falling faster
the shadows whisper
and rain spatters
like death's downpour:

'Fight for me, dawn-slayer,
wake with me, sleep-sower,
keeper of dreams,
the dream we came for.'

There is no noise.
Only the quick
paws of the cat in the dark
like feet on the stairs,

but the cold grey hands of the sea clap
on the beached long-ships,
and a shape pours itself flat
to the chink of sword music.

Viking cat in the dark
is paw-licked velvet, sinew of shadow.
A thread of smoke, bitterly burning
quivers her body like a riddle.

Baby sleep

's
not like any other
day sleep   night sleep
long drive sleep
too cold   too hot sleep
What's that window doing shut?   sleep
get a bit of peace sleep
hungry   thirsty
need to pee
sleep,

baby sleep's
all over the shop sleep
new nappy and babygro poppers
done up to the neck sleep
fat fingers
starfishing
damp feathers
on neck curling
baby lotion and talc sleep
sleep in Mum and Dad's bed sleep
cry in sleep and then sleep sleep
sleep while the big peop
le wash and dress sleep
baby sleep

Frostbite

When you grow tired of the flame
wumping to life in the central heating boiler,
and the duvet sweats like obstinate flesh
in the middle of winter,

don't finger the lightswitch. Leave the coil
of electricity sleeping. Go down
tread after tread by the draught
of heat coming upward. The voice

of the house is warning. *Get out*
it breathes, *Leave us alone*
to our shuffling of dust-mites, our sorting
of smell and shadow into home.

First the bolt, then the chain, then the Chubb.
You're outside, but even in a nightdress
that comes to the thighs, you can't rub the warmth off.

Basketball player on Pentecost Monday

With his hands he teaches wind to move –
not this shuffle of leaves
from rows of pollarded trees
but the salt–laden, incoming
breath of the Indies.

He's six foot seven,
liquid in dull grey track suit,
his trainers undone.
There's a small keen boy
at his heels, yapping
for ball-time, air-time.
It's playtime in the gardens
with children sagely going round
on patient horses they strike with small
privileged hands.

Behind him, gravelly sand,
a guitarist picking
the bones of a tune
mournful as Sunday,
the empty horses
of carousels turning.

Tell the basketball player how tight
time is, how he's reached perfection
at the same time as the man with his rake
puts the gravel straight on something.
Tell him this is the moment
the arrow of his life flew out of
to return into his breastbone.
Or say nothing.

Tiger lookout

Refrigerator days.
Ours is the size of a walk-in larder,
casing everything.

One word
which has gone out of fashion
is *putrefaction*.

When Simmonds fell from his tiger lookout
it was not the growl
nor the stripes
that said *tiger*.

It was the tiger's breath.
All that old, bad meat
furring its teeth.

For a moment Simmonds was critical,
sniffing the exhalation of corpses,
the walk-in larder where he was going.

Tiger Moth caterpillar

Two spines curve in
as the sisters face on a gate
in their matching cardigans.

They are looking into something –
a stolen Swan Vesta box
plump with green privet,

and there's one match left
with which to poke it –
their marvellous possession.

Inner thighs chafe on a crust of lichen.
Riding the gate is the best game
these two have ever come on.

The more bloody a ballad
they more they love it. Cigars,
betrayal, the flames of hell

and the slaughter of innocence
are what speaks, makes the gate creak.
Girls, give us a song

in your tidy cardigans. Your hair's
deceptively sleek, you are
tangled, complicit, in on it.

Hungry Thames

Hungry Thames, I walk over the bridge
half-scared you'll whittle me down

where the brown water is eager
and tipped with foam.

You sigh and suck. You lick at the steps
you would like to come up.

Hungry Thames, we feed you on concrete,
orange-peel, polystyrene cups,

we hold our kids by a handful of clothing
to let them look at your dimples,

your smiling waters. We should hold them tighter,
these are whirlpools, this is hunger

lashing its tail in the mud, deep down
where the river gets what it wants.

The wasp

Now winter comes and I am half-asleep
crawling the hollow of an apple, my sound
a battery toy in a child's cupped hand,

or I climb to a ledge and lie, dulled
by its half-warmth. Half-wasp, I'm still
helpless not to sting your exploring finger

helpless in the pulse of my body.
The paddle of your hand churns
as you find something to kill me.

I keep on stinging. I cannot learn
through my crispness, the coat of warning
that says what I am.

Little Ellie and the timeshare salesman

The man who gave little Ellie his forever
love was a timeshare salesman.
He let her look round the place
when the carpet was freshly steam-cleaned
and the teabag box was full to the brim,
but he left little Ellie for an instant
and she spied the used teabag jam-jar
sodden and rusty as iron.

Oh Ellie, whispered little Ellie,
there have been many here before you.
But she was smiling at the door
when he gave her his hand, wet from the ballcock
he'd quickly fixed in the cistern.
In a serenade of gurgles and yawns
the plumbing talked itself down
and perfect Ellie was his dream.

How could he replace or kill her
with her genius for noticing nothing
but the nice day, the short walk to the pool
the view of the beach from the bathroom window?
Sweet Ellie never crossed the time-share salesman,
but tended her one week like a garden.
She did not keep a diary where the others
might be noted or brooded over.

Kindly she watches him run on the wheel
of his weeks till he gets back to nineteen
where she is always happy to wait for him.
Dusty geraniums come back to life
in the days where Ellie waters them,
and the time-share salesman slackens his smiles
at the sight of Ellie's daring paëlla:
in week nineteen she is his forever.

Bouncing boy

(for Paul)

All the squares of trampoline are taken
by children leaping like chessmen
who won't play the game. Up, flying.
from tiny freeholds, hitting the sky's
elastic surprise, then down.

There's a space for you always.
Two kids eating ice-cream
with careful darts of the tongue
watch as you start to climb
the icy November sky, hand over hand.

You hear the clap of the sea
and your bright blue trampoline applauding
with the dull fervour of rubber
each time you go down,

and the kids eating ice-cream
with wind in their teeth say nothing
as the time mounts and your turn
grows impossibly long.

Tea at Brandt's

Music plays gently. Yesterday's morning paper
flutters at the end of its long emigration
from being news. This is the present,

but when? Coconut cake, a stained napkin,
a tea-glass bisected by long spoon.
Any minute now it's going to rain.

What kind of animal is the past?
A wooden screen makes two rooms of one.
On the other side, where I saw her last,

my baby girl. I'll wipe her nose with the napkin,
take her to the Ladies and change her,
blow the bubble of words towards her
that says, *This is the present, there is no other.*

We are men, not beasts

We are men, not beasts
though we fall in the dark
on the rattlesnake's path
and flinch with fire of fear
running over our flesh
and beat it to death,

we are men, not beasts
and we walk upright
with the moss-feathered dark
like a shawl on our shoulders
and we carry fire
steeply, inside a cage of fingers,

we are men, not beasts,
and what we cannot help wanting
we banish – the barn yawn, the cow breath,
the stickiness we come from.

Index of titles and first lines

(Titles are shown in italics, first lines in roman type.)

255